T0001606

Beyond
Tidy

Beyond Tidy

Declutter Your Mind and Discover the Magic of Organized Living

8 Powerful Principles for Creating a Life You Love

Annmarie Brogan and Marie Limpert
of Organize Me! of NY, LLC

Racehorse Publishing

Racehorse Publishing books may be purchased in bulk at special discounts for sales promotion, corporate gifts, fund-raising, or educational purposes. Special editions can also be created to specifications. For details, contact the Special Sales Department, Sky Pony Press, 307 West 36th Street, 11th Floor, New York, NY 10018 or info@skyhorsepublishing.com.

Racehorse Publishing™ is a pending trademark of Skyhorse Publishing, Inc.®, a Delaware corporation.

Visit our website at www.skyponypress.com.

10 9 8 7 6 5 4 3 2

Library of Congress Control Number: 2020933978

Cover design by Daniel Brount
Cover artwork by Getty Images
Author photograph by Bryan Leale

Print ISBN: 978-1-63158-603-3
Ebook ISBN: 978-1-63158-604-0

Printed in the United States of America

To our beautiful friend Marcy, who gave us the not-so-gentle nudge we needed to take a chance and start our own business. Thank you for your love and friendship, and for believing in us. We miss your smile and the light you brought to this world.

Table of Contents

Introduction

and emotional well-being. It's not just about the way things appear on the surface. There is an implication of renewal: the opportunity to rein-habit your space, to reclaim territory, and overcome any frustration and confusion about being organized. Plus, our emphasis is on positive and impactful language. We want to take a book that's organizational, pick it up a little bit, and make it personal, inspirational, and fun. We're ready to play!

Congratulations! If you are reading this, then you have hope. You believe, even to the smallest degree, that you can learn to be more organized and change the way things currently are. More importantly, you believe that you can play a direct role in making that change. There can be no change without hope, so even if this book is your "Hail Mary" play, you're still in the game and we celebrate you!

When we were first approached about writing a book, it was important to stay true to ourselves as teachers of organizing strategies. We have been professional organizers for thirteen years, and in that time we've worked hard to craft proven systems and language that motivates and resonates with those who come to us for help. There are many organizing books out there, so what do we offer that's different than the others? What can we bring to the party that causes a tangible "shift" for you, the reader?

What makes us unique is our emphasis on the "why" behind all the "whats" we are asking you to do. We want you to understand the impact behind each tip, strategy, and suggestion. By *impact* we mean how your life and circumstances will be positively affected, including improvements in your state of mind and emotional well-being. It's not just about the way things appear on the outside. There is an abundance of research that supports the benefits of cultivating positivity, increasing optimism and hope, and staying motivated. *This book is a fusion of our best organizing principles with positive and behavioral psychology*. While the primary focus is on organizing, we sprinkle the research throughout the book in an easily digestible way to support the principles we teach. We believe that when you combine conceptual understanding with tangible, proven strategies, you will be equipped to handle any organizing challenge.

In other words, we go "beyond tidy" to a much higher level.

To begin, we reflected a lot on the many different reasons people have called us over the years. The range of demographics, circumstances, and physical/mental health challenges that make up and affect our client base would probably surprise you. Yet the negative emotions attached to feeling disorganized are consistent across all of the above factors.

One thing is clear: there are many reasons why people are disorganized. Some have simply never been organized. Maybe they were raised in a cluttered and chaotic environment, where things were always out of place. Perhaps they never learned good strategies at home or at school. Some truly believe they weren't blessed with the "organizing gene" and therefore aren't innately organized. They call us when their disorganization is adversely affecting their lives, work, and/or relationships and something needs to change.

Others struggle with mental health challenges, such as depression, anxiety, or ADHD, which make it truly difficult to stay focused and on task. They come to us to simplify their lives and learn techniques for making things more manageable.

Then there are those who have always been super organized until a life event gets them off track (think: death of a loved one, birth of a child, need to go back to work, unexpected job loss, etc.). Not used to feeling out of control and scattered, mastering their "new normal" becomes top of the priority list.

Combine this with different personalities, circumstances, and family dynamics and it's obvious that a one size fits all approach isn't effective. However, the more we reflected, the clearer it became that our clients' successes over the years have been rooted in key unifying factors:

We come to you without judgement.

As we just mentioned, there are a lot of reasons why people get to a point where they feel they need our help. Our clients learn quickly that our goal is to empower and help them move forward. This calls for more than just teaching tips and tricks, although we've got plenty of them! It requires feeling free from perceived judgement (including self-judgement), which often renders people immobile and unable to take that first step. We invite you to come to this process with self-compassion. Give yourself permission to be human as you navigate new ways to approach organization, leaving any self-judgement at the door.

We work as a team.

We are teachers, motivators, collaborators, and strategists. While we feel becoming more organized will lead to greater self-esteem, our energy is spent helping to increase your self-*effi-cacy*, the belief in your abilities to handle challenges and complete tasks successfully. We believe in your resourcefulness, even though you may be feeling quite incapable and out of control. When people truly feel safe and supported, they are free to take risks and try new things. They become excited to explore and learn. As your teammates, we help you increase positive emotions in order to build curiosity and openness to what's possible. As Dr. Barbara Frederickson explains in her book, *Positivity*, "Positivity broadens our minds and expands our range of vision . . . A broad mind changes the way you think and act in a wide range of circumstances. When you see more, more ideas come to mind, more actions become possible." Positive emotions "broaden and build" and cause "upward spirals" that filter into other areas of life. Think of it as a positive chain reaction.[1]

We build trust.

We understand how emotional and overwhelming life can be when a person is disorganized, especially when he/she begins to "unpack" the underlying causes of his/her disorganization. Our clients trust us with so much more than just their physical belongings. They also share their feelings, emotions, insecurities, and secrets—the things that make them most vulnerable. We get to see sides of them they don't share with their closest family and friends. We do not take that trust for granted, and we come to each project with compassion and respect.

Conversely, part of the way in which we empower our clients is through *our* trust in *their* capabilities. We believe wholeheartedly that anyone who comes to us with a sincere desire to improve their situation can learn what we have to teach. If they are willing to shift their mindset and establish new behavior patterns, they can and will achieve organizing success.

So perhaps the most powerful gift we offer is this: Throughout the process, we cultivate a "growth mindset"—a belief that talent and ability are not "fixed," but merely starting points for what's possible with hard work, dedicated practice, and a sincere desire to learn. It is human nature to compare ourselves to others, and the disorganized person often feels like everyone else has it all together. But don't let a "fixed mindset" stop you! This is not an "either you have the 'organizing gene' or you don't" situation. Dr. Carol Dweck of Stanford University says, "Just because some people can do something with little or no training, it doesn't mean that others can't do it (and sometimes do it even better) with training."[2]

We help our clients reframe negative, limiting thoughts and beliefs into positive, curious, and more solution-focused ones.

So how does all this translate from working with us in person to what you will find in this book? We begin by answering this question with two more (which definitely would have annoyed our parents growing up!):

What if we were to tell you that being organized isn't what you might think it is? What if we begged you, just for a little while, to stop looking at those jaw dropping pictures of (seemingly) organized perfection on Pinterest? (No really . . . Stop looking at Pinterest. Pinterest is only a surface look at what your space and life could be. It does not reflect what the inner state of "being" organized actually means.)

Simply put, organizing is knowing what you have and where to find it when you need it.

It means *not wasting time and money replacing things you already own because you can't find them.* It means *being reliable and on time for appointments since getting ready to go out no longer feels like competing in an Olympic event.* It means *taking the space you have and getting the most out of it.* It means *managing your energy for more important decisions and tasks, which gives you better emotional regulation and willpower.* The bottom line? It means *creating a life that you LOVE—one that has been deliberately designed by you, rather than a life that is simply a byproduct of the chaos around you.*

Organized people are resilient. They have strategies and a Plan B for when unexpected things come up. They aren't fully derailed and they remain confident and optimistic that they can get back on track quickly. In fact, research shows that those who plan for how they will implement their goals triple their chances of success! This is true even for difficult goals.[3]

Organizing is not how "neat and tidy" something looks on the outside. We've seen many a pristine-looking home that has chaos lurking behind every cabinet door. Rather, it's how the set-up and layout of your drawers, cabinets, and closets *support the way you and your family want to live.*

For example, both of us have very organized kitchens with a specific flow, but each kitchen is tailored to the unique needs of our families. One of us has an aging parent who tries to sneak foods he isn't supposed to eat. So certain foods need to be kept up high and out of reach because she can't trust him! The other one of us keeps those same foods in plain sight because it's not an issue with her family. We often say, "There is no right or wrong way to organize, as long as there's an organized way."

We tailor organizing solutions to the unique personalities, needs and circumstances of our clients. However, there are basic principles that we teach *all* of our clients, and these principles are what we focus on here. And the best part is that even though mastering these principles can have a profound impact on your life, they are actually very simple to learn and implement!

If disorganization is affecting your quality of life and preventing you from showing up in the world the way that you want to—confidently, reliably, and with an abundance of positive energy—then this book is for you.

What you can expect:
Each chapter will cover one of our Top Eight Organizing Principles:

- What it is, in easy-to-understand language
- Why it's important/how it will impact you
- What it will save you (time/money/energy/space)

We will also include personal stories, favorite social media posts, and mini case studies from our real-life clients.

These chapters are designed to help you understand not only *what* to do, but also *why* we recommend it and *how* it will impact you. This is so important in keeping you motivated and empowered.

Although mastering any one of these principles can have a positive effect, we will show you how once you master them all, you can interweave them into seamless and effortless organizing systems that help you create a home and life you love.

We are honored to be on this journey with you.

Happy Organizing!
Annmarie and Marie

PART I

CREATING YOUR MINDSET

CHAPTER 1

Change on the Outside Must Begin with Change on the Inside

Deep, huh? You may be thinking, "I signed up for tangible organizing tips, not New Age philosophy." Yet, there's no way around it. We must start with this idea, because if you aren't willing to reset your thinking and change your behavior, none of the rest will matter.

Wanting to be organized is not enough.

There is controversy over whether or not Einstein really offered his own definition of insanity, but it's true nevertheless:

"Insanity is doing the same thing over and over again, but expecting different results."

If you keep [cleaning/straightening/organizing] and things always go back to the way they were, it's because:

- Something you're doing isn't working
- There's something you're *not* doing, OR
- There's something you're not doing *consistently*.

No matter what, the key is to change your mindset.

Mindset affects your behavior, which then in turn reinforces your mindset. They are connected. Therefore, you can't fully learn the organizing principles that will drive new behaviors and habits without first exploring your innate belief system. Let us show you how changing your mindset first is the key to unlocking your inner organizational "gene"-ius (see what we did there?).

Our thoughts are very powerful. They are the lens through which we see the world, and the underlying factor behind how we react to situations and events in our lives. They also determine what, if any, action we take in response. This is a main reason why two people can experience the same exact situation yet react very differently.

Years ago, we worked with a schoolteacher who was divorced and living with her young son. She called us because the clutter in her house had gotten out of control. The disorganization was causing her significant anxiety. In fact, she said it was "sucking the life out of her." During the session, she confided that she had grown up in a family where things were never thrown out. Turns out, her parents had lived through The Great Depression, where food was scarce and the option to buy new things wasn't always viable. Old clothing was given to other family members or made into other items, such as rags or pillows. Broken gadgets and appliances were kept for parts, in case such parts could ever be repurposed. They made do with what they had and came up with creative ways to repurpose everything so it never went to waste.

Even after the Depression ended, this mindset prevailed and shaped the way her parents lived long after they could well afford what they needed. Donating was hard, despite the idea that their unused things could go to the less fortunate. Perhaps because they had *been* the less fortunate, they couldn't bear to part with anything they acquired, for any reason. Even letting go of broken items was painfully difficult. The stuff they held onto took valuable space away from other, more used items, and as a result, they lived in a cluttered and uninviting home.

Our client, on the other hand, held a different mindset. She believed that clutter was a barrier to living a better, easier-to-manage life. She couldn't fathom why anyone would want to keep several broken vacuum cleaners or stained clothing that didn't even fit. Far from causing anxiety, setting aside things for donation made her feel lighter and more in control of her space. Putting broken items in the garbage was a no-brainer.

What *was* causing her anxiety was the fact that for a variety of reasons, her house had started to resemble her childhood home. She did not want her son to grow up in that environment or develop her parents' mindset about his belongings. This is what prompted her to call us.

Two different belief systems. Two very different ways of approaching (and reacting to) the organizing process.

Henry Ford famously said: "Whether you think you can or think you can't, you're right."

If you hold a strong belief that you can never learn to be organized or nothing you do will matter, it will be difficult to stay open to new suggestions or maintain a good level of motivation.

In contrast, if you hold a strong belief that it **is** possible to learn and improve new skills with dedication and practice, you will be more likely to stay the course and keep moving forward even when you encounter obstacles.

Research studies in the field of neuroplasticity have shown that the brain is very malleable and adaptive. Every time you learn something new, neurons or nerve cells in the brain "fire up" and create new neural pathways. You are literally rewiring your brain to adapt to new information and situations. You are changing both the structure and the functionality of your brain.[4]

The implications of this are incredibly exciting and go far beyond what we will cover here. For our purposes, it means that it is biologically possible to change the way we think, and therefore how we see the world. It also means that with dedication and effort, we can learn new skills, develop better habits, and create a different way of interacting with our environment and the people in it.

That is something *big* to celebrate! Even if you've always believed that you could never get better at organization (or any skill for that matter), science is proving that theory wrong!

According to Dr. Carol Dweck, a leading researcher on the topic of mindset, there are two main types: a "fixed" mindset and a "growth" mindset. Those with a fixed mindset believe that their abilities, intelligence, and talent are set in stone and can't be developed. They view the need to put forth effort as a sign of low talent or ability. Therefore, they avoid challenges that might expose them as deficient. In contrast, people with a growth mindset believe that their basic abilities are just the foundation, and can be developed and cultivated through hard work, dedication, and practice. They view challenges, and even failures, as opportunities to learn and improve.[5]

We believe that a growth mindset is essential for success and for living a happier, more flourishing life. So our approach is always to work from a place of curiosity and possibility. We want you to think in terms of what you are *building and creating*, not what you are *giving up or losing.* The first way feels much more empowering and purposeful; the second feels stressful and demotivating. We encourage you to be an active creator of your dream life, and there's no room for negativity in the process.

Therefore, the first step in this process is to start paying attention to your mind chatter. We don't know about you, but there are a lot of thoughts that race through our heads throughout the day. Can you relate? What are your thoughts telling you, and are they serving you in reaching your goals? On any given day, would you say your thoughts are more positive or negative?

A single, negative thought is one thing. We all have negative thoughts that pop up here and there. However, repeated thoughts become our beliefs. And when those beliefs are negative, limiting and/or self-sabotaging, they can create quite a bit of chaos. It is very important to note that negative thoughts aren't necessarily accurate thoughts, which is why they should be challenged! We want to become aware of the narrative in our head, so we can talk back to negative thoughts and reframe them.

So how can we change negative thoughts? Sadly, we can't just toss them out the window. We can't "unthink" our thoughts. We can only replace them with better feeling and better serving ones. The more we repeat these better thoughts, the stronger they become and the more they become etched in our brain— literally and figuratively. As they do, the negative thoughts become weaker and weaker and have much less of an impact. Thank you, neuroplasticity![6]

This is, of course, easier said than done. We are biologically wired to place greater emphasis on the negative. In positive psychology, this is referred to as our negativity bias, and we all have it.[7] Centuries ago, it's what kept our ancestors safe from threats to their survival. We still have that same wiring, but it affects us differently in today's world. Here's an easy-to-understand example: If we receive feedback on a project or performance and someone says five positive things and one negative thing, what do most people hone in on? The one negative thing, and sometimes to the *complete exclusion* of the positive things also mentioned.

We have a client who begins every session by telling us everything she hasn't done or kept up with since we last saw her. Without fail, throughout the session we learn all the things she *has* accomplished and maintained and it is often a looooooong list. She is an absolute rockstar, but her negativity bias game is strong. It's something she is working on, and we support her by ending each session with a recap of everything she has accomplished.

That's why we always encourage our clients and followers to "celebrate the wins!" It's not just about the end result; it's about the different ways we learn and grow throughout the journey. That's what keeps us in a more positive frame of mind, and more willing to try things we might not have considered before.

The reality is, there are many different ways to approach an organizing project, and there are factors that are unique to each family. Sometimes it takes a few tries to get things right, so having a growth mindset is key to navigating the process and not giving up.

We are also believers in affirmations and expressing our goals in the positive, preferably in language that suggests what you desire has already happened or is happening.

- "I am organized and reaching my goals."
- "I am on top of my finances and my paperwork."
- "I have good systems in place so my house doesn't become cluttered."
- "I am learning new ways to make my household run more smoothly."
- "I am proud of how far I have come."
- "Every day I am improving."
- "Every day I am one step closer to reaching my goals."
- "When I have a setback, I trust in my ability to handle it."
- "I have an effective and reliable Plan B."
- "I am as prepared as I can be."

What affirmations can you come up with on your own?

Bottom line: Believe you can. Commit to change. Proactively take down negative mind chatter. Move forward fearlessly!

Allow us to offer a few more thoughts before we get to our top organizing principles. Although the systems we offer our clients are tailored to their specific needs and vision, these are basic things to keep in mind as you embark on this adventure:

Reset your thinking
Remember, the clutter and disorganization likely did not happen overnight, so it is unreasonable to think that it could be

erased overnight. Understand that this will be an ever-changing journey, and there will be steps forward and back along the way. The steps back can provide valuable insight and opportunities for self-discovery. This is why a growth mindset is so important. Reflecting back on the past has the potential to make you feel bad about how things may have gotten to this point. It's perfectly natural to have feelings of discomfort and unease. Having self-compassion will allow you to move through the reflection without being weighed down by negativity.

Self-reflection can be good—and healthy—when it is done from a place of curiosity and with an intention to move forward. What wasn't working before? What got in the way? What did work and is still working? What would you like to change moving forward? How would making positive changes impact different areas of your life? Focus on what can be *learned*, and how you can use this information to create a space and life that aligns with your values and desires.

Long walk, baby steps

This is particularly important for those who are in an extreme state of disorganization. If you view this as one big project, you are going to get overwhelmed and subsequently discouraged. You will feel bad about yourself. This journey is not about self-loathing, self-judgment, or "what ifs?" It's about being in the present and learning from past mistakes to shape a better and happier future. Very rarely does everything go one hundred percent smoothly the first time. You will try some perfectly good systems that simply don't work for you and your family. These are just setbacks, not failures. Another difference between a growth and fixed mindset is how a person perceives failure. A person with a fixed mindset says, "I'm a failure" and uses that as an excuse for not trying anymore. The failure is viewed as validation that they are not good enough. A person with a growth mindset says, "I've failed this time around. What can I learn from this? What can I do differently next time?" The failure is viewed as an opportunity to grow.[8]

So don't give up if you try a few things and they don't work. With each attempt, you will learn a little more about yourself, your family, and how to approach the organizing process. Eventually, you will hit upon what works for you—and it will be worth your patience and effort!

Keep the inner and outer conversation positive

As you become organized, you will feel excited and hopeful. You will feel other emotions, too. Many clients express remorse and sadness that they "allowed" things to get out of control. Don't focus on those negative emotions; they will only impede your progress. Focus on the fact that you have committed to turning things around and are making progress! You must be your first motivator, and then surround yourself with others who support you.

Speaking of which, don't be surprised if all of your hard work doesn't spark the validation and gratitude from your family as you hope it will! Our clients have received a variety of responses to their organizing efforts:

- *No reaction at all*—say what? That's right! Some clients have worked their butts off to get a room decluttered or their paperwork in order, only to have their spouse or children come home and not notice anything looks different! Even when told about the organizing, the spouse or children say, "It looks the same," or "Looks like nothing got done." They don't recognize it as the huge undertaking it was. This is very disheartening, and a real downer after the "high" of organizing success!

    No one can understand the process unless they go through it. Some people think organizing means throwing everything out. So if they see a room full of stuff, they think nothing has changed. However, *you* know what's changed. You know the work you've put in. Now you know exactly what you have and where to find it. You can access it easily. Your space is being used more efficiently and you have more control.

- *Anxiety/paranoia*—did those ladies touch my stuff? Where is everything? How much did all of this cost? Shouldn't you be able to do this on your own?

- *Insecurity/defensiveness*—after all, *you* getting organized makes *their* disorganization more apparent. They might outwardly put down or downright sabotage the work you've been doing. We know. We've witnessed it, and it makes staying motivated and focused that much harder. That's why it's important you not start this process for anyone or anything other than your own desire to make positive changes. You can't control other people's reactions and behavior. You can, however, set a positive tone right from the beginning.

Try to get your loved ones on board before you begin

Unless you live alone, your journey will both affect and be affected by those around you. Sometimes the initial negative reactions come from a place of feeling blindsided or that they didn't have a say in the matter. Much of this resistance might be relieved by having a family meeting before you start the process, in order to alleviate any confusion or fears your loved ones may have.

Tell them why this is important to you. Explain how it can positively impact the family and household. Let them know you understand that this will affect them, too. This will show respect for their feelings and hopefully put them in a more excited and positive frame of mind as you begin the process. Really listen to what they have to say and what their concerns are. Patiently answer any questions they may have. You want them to come on board willingly. However, even if that doesn't happen, don't let it stop you from starting with your own stuff. Your initiative may inspire them to jump on board as they see the positive impact it has on you firsthand.

Of course, there is also the very real possibility that your family will love and appreciate what you are trying to do right from the start! They will openly embrace the changes and happily help out! That is always the hope, since you multiply your chances of success and significantly cut down how long your projects will take when everyone is invested and engaged.

As new systems are put in place and things are given a proper home, it's important that you consistently and respectfully communicate these changes and *why* they will make life better for all of you. Don't expect your family members to "get it" after being told only once. Otherwise, you are setting them up to fail, and you are undermining your own achievement! Remember, they are not mind (or mindset) readers! Try your best to be patient as they too learn new behaviors and habits, and show them and yourself compassion along the way.

These are just a few basic concepts that will help you reach your goals. Next let's explore the million-dollar question: "Where do I begin?"

CHAPTER 2
Where Do I Begin?

If it were easy, we'd all be super organized, and probably at our goal weight, too!

Actually, in the beginning, getting organized is a lot like trying to lose weight. Many of our clients come to us wanting a "magic pill," a quick way to turn everything around. But just like with weight loss, there is no magic pill. To be successful at either, you have to focus, commit to changing certain behaviors, and develop good and consistent habits.

The thought of all this can be exhausting in and of itself, especially for those who start out in a severe state of disorganization. It all just seems insurmountable and the number one question is often, "Where do I even begin?"

Most of the time the answer is to hone in on what it is that causes you the most *stress*, and then start there.

Stress manifests itself in many ways. You can feel it physically in your body—rapid heartbeat, sweaty palms, feelings of anxiety. You can experience negative emotions such as shame and embarrassment. Stress may cause you to snap at others in anger or frustration—or to shut down completely and retreat into a state of complete *inaction*.

There is an established relationship between disorganization and stress levels. The more things seem out of control, the higher your stress level and the lower your productivity will be (which leads to more stress).[9] Do you see how quickly the negative spiral starts?

When you are ready for real change, ask yourself these two questions:

1. What is causing me the most stress and affecting my daily life *now*?
2. Which area, if improved, would have the biggest and most immediate impact on my day-to-day life?

That's where you start. The clutter in the spare bedroom might really irk you, but is it wreaking havoc on daily productivity? Or is it the lack of a proper system for handling incoming bills, school paperwork, and/or financial records? Or the fact that every cabinet in your kitchen is jammed so full that getting anything out of them puts you at risk of injury by avalanche?

Sometimes our clients come to us wanting to work on one area, but once they start focusing on how their different areas of disorganization make them *feel*, they decide to switch their order of priority.

In addition to relieving stress, it's also best to focus on improving the area that will have the most impact on your daily life. Every family is different. For one, it might be the kitchen—the hub of the home—the place where everything is handled, from food prep to homework to bills/paperwork. Having a good flow is key, especially when multiple people are using the space! For another family, it might be getting the kids' bedrooms in order to foster independence and responsibility, as well as a good environment for healthy sleep habits.

Are there exceptions to these rules? Of course! Sometimes many areas need to be worked on, but a deadline necessitates working on one area before the others. A few examples of this are:

- You unexpectedly need to host out-of-town guests, but your spare bedroom has become your dumping ground for everything you don't know what to do with. At the moment, you can't even walk in there. Even though other rooms or categories might need attention, this room becomes the priority because there is a deadline attached to it—your guests are arriving in a few days!

- You are involved in a lawsuit or court case and need to gather specific paperwork. We have had several clients who needed our support in divorce and childcare proceedings. Having solid, irrefutable evidence in writing helped them immensely. As in the first example, there are deadlines related to such matters. Plus, there are financial and emotional gains/losses contingent upon the outcome. So this would take priority over other areas at this time.

- You wish to use your attic to store things you still want but aren't using regularly. Awesome, they don't need to be in your main space! *But*, the attic is filled to the brim with things you haven't seen or looked at in ten years. In fact, you really have no idea what's up there. It's a great space that could hold a *lot*, but it can't fit a single other thing. In this case, we would suggest getting this area in order first and then having it ready to house things that are cluttering up the rest of your home.

If you are still unsure of where to begin, here's another strategy you can try. We recommend that you do a physical walk-through of your home, room by room, to help prioritize organizing projects. Jot down notes regarding each room and what specifically needs to be organized within it (a.k.a. a "Take Action" List). You can use a notebook or the notes app on your phone. Either way, writing things down is an effective way to declutter your mind and stay focused. It brings a bit of order to chaos, both mentally and physically, so you can hone in more accurately on where to begin.

As you enter each room to make your "Take Action" list, ask yourself these three questions:

1. What feelings do I carry deep inside when I walk in here?

If you feel anxious, overwhelmed, angry, or just plain unhappy when you open the door, then this may be one of your contenders. Try to be as specific as possible. Is it the whole room that makes you feel this way, or one particular area?

2. Do I have a specific budget? Will this organizing project require only your time/labor, or will it be more extensive, requiring new furniture or construction?
   Being realistic about the financial component may bump certain projects further down on the priority list.

3. What is my timeframe? Do I have a limited amount of time to get the project done?
   Time constraints might impact the priority of certain projects. Estimate how much time you need versus how much time you can devote to tackling this space.

Once you have the answers to these three questions for each room/space/project on your list, then prioritize accordingly.

And if you are still not sure after that, it may be in your best interest to schedule a consultation with a professional organizer. Even if you wish to do the organizing yourself, having an expert evaluate your situation may save you a lot of time and money in the long run.

There may not be a magic pill, but a focused and committed "slow and steady" approach will win you the race. Sometimes figuring out the best place to start is half the battle! When you couple a starting point with a positive growth mindset, you come out of the gate with your eye on the win! As you gradually regain control, it will feel fabulous, exciting, energizing, and empowering. And that's the best kind of magic!

CHAPTER 3

Wrapping Your Head Around Clutter

According to professional organizer Andrew Mellen, clutter is "nothing more than deferred decisions . . . individual choices you didn't make then that are now piled up one on top of the other."[10]

We definitely agree, with the exception of the "nothing more" part. Deferred decisions most certainly do result in clutter. There's a difference between clutter and stuff that just hasn't been put away. The majority of clutter is homeless—it has no designated place to return to each day. It is a deferred decision that results in things being where they don't belong, such as on the floor, hanging off the railing, or shoved in the closet.

An example of a deferred decision: "I don't know if I'm keeping this new shirt, so I'll leave it in the bag on the living room floor until I decide . . ." In this state of limbo, that bag is clutter. The sooner you decide if you are keeping it or returning it, the quicker you will eliminate the rise of clutter.

"Deferred Decision" clutter affects everyone and often looks messy.

However, there is also a category of clutter that is not the result of deferred decisions. These are items you have very intentionally decided to keep. They may even have a designated spot within your home, where they are out of sight and "minding their own business." These items don't look like clutter, but they are the reason clutter has built up in other areas of your home. Yes, you read that correctly. These items are not needed and not being used, yet are taking up valuable space that you could be using for the things you do need.

We propose that, for some families, these things tucked away in the closet are actually clutter, *despite how neat and tidy they look*. This is because the space they take up makes it seem like there isn't enough space to store other things. When this leads to deferred decisions on things you do need and use, then the cycle of disorganization strengthens.

We have written this chapter to inspire you to really think about all the ways clutter shows up in our homes and lives. It is much more than just the physical mess we see, and it goes beyond the obvious examples of clutter that automatically come to mind. We break it down into three categories: Clutter by Type, Clutter by Location, and Clutter by Reason. Then there is Mental Clutter, which as some of you already know is in a category all by itself!

Let's talk now about clutter, so we can then spend the rest of our time together discussing how to get rid of it!

Clutter by Type

Here are common types of clutter and a few examples for each. Which ones resonate the most with you?

- **Paper clutter:** coupons that we clip and save but forget to bring with us to the store; bills that have been paid but not filed; store receipts that we accumulate and then dump somewhere, like the kitchen counter; emails that we print as a reference or reminder to take action but then are forgotten about in a pile.

- **Mail clutter:** mail that is brought into the house that sits on the kitchen counter or hallway table for days without being opened; junk mail and envelopes from opened mail that are not discarded.

- **Book/magazine/newspaper/catalog clutter:** items that were never read or if read, haven't yet been recycled. This includes free or paid subscriptions that are delivered daily, weekly, or monthly that pile up because life gets too hectic and we don't commit to reading them in a timely way.

- **Medicine cabinet clutter:** prescriptions not finished and/or no longer needed; expired meds.

- **Laundry clutter:** dirty and unsorted laundry that gets thrown together on the floor; clothing you did manage to wash and dry that is temporarily living in the basket because it was never folded or put away; the collection of single socks that every family has.

- **Pantry clutter:** cooking items bought for the latest food trend that are not used and then expire; extra quantities of non-perishable items that we don't consume fast enough and then expire.
- **Fridge clutter:** leftovers that get pushed to the back and forgotten about; extra quantities of perishable items that we don't consume fast enough and then expire; magnets, sticky notes, pictures, reminder cards haphazardly affixed to the outside fridge doors.
- **Toy clutter:** toys the kids have outgrown or are no longer interested in playing with; toys and games with broken or missing pieces that are "unplayable" but still in your home.
- **Clothing/accessories clutter:** outdated; wrong sizes; old looking; just not your style any longer but are still taking up space in your drawers and closet (or worse, the floor and other surfaces).
- **Unfinished projects clutter:** crafts and scrapbooks that were started but never completed; unused photo albums bought to store printed pictures.
- **Children's school paper clutter:** everyday drawings that you feel guilty throwing out because your child brought them home from school; homework; tests; projects; artwork.
- **Jewelry clutter:** pieces that are broken or no longer desired that you haven't gotten rid of yet, making it challenging to find the pieces you do want to wear.

- **Electronic (hardware) clutter:** DVDs and CDs not being used; broken cases; loose or scratched discs; VHS/ camcorder videos; old cameras, cell phones, video cameras, phone accessories, cable and USB wires, etc.
- **Digital (software) clutter:** never-ending text/email/ social media notifications; read and unread text messages and group chats that haven't been addressed or deleted; in-boxes filled with work, personal, promotional and informational emails that haven't been deleted or sorted into digital folders; unsorted and unfiled documents and photos.

Clutter by Location

Anything out of place in a particular room or space becomes *that space's clutter*, regardless of which *type* of clutter it is. This is often the result of the random dumping we do when we are 1) avoiding the decision about what to do with it or, 2) convinced we don't have enough time to put it away. We call this "For Now" Clutter (more on this later in the chapter). So we can have paper clutter in the living room or toy clutter in the kitchen. There are many possible combinations, and we have seen most of them over the years!

Popular spaces to dump "deferred decisions":

- Attic
- Basement
- Garage

- Spare Bedroom
- Home Office/Desk
- Car
- Dining Room Table
- Drawers
- Under the Bed
- Briefcases/Handbags/Wallets

These are just a few examples, but really clutter can be in any room or space within your home. Also, the same clutter in one person's basement may appear in another person's attic. Either way, these things wouldn't be clutter if they had a designated home to return to or weren't items you no longer use taking space from the things you do.

Take a tour of your home and the different spaces within it. Which are the ones where you have clutter?

Clutter by Reason

The following categories are clutter because of the reasons why you are keeping them. We go more in-depth with these because we believe their negative effects are highly underestimated (and often flat-out unrecognized):

"For Now" Clutter

Years ago, we wrote a blog post on this subject, not realizing we might one day include it in a book! The quick suggestions at the end have been expanded in later chapters:

"For Now"—two of the most frustrating words an organizer can hear . . .

It seems unlikely that six letters could come together to cause actual havoc, but we assure you they can. Because what they represent is a refusal to make a decision or follow through on a task. And the worst part? We're supposed to believe it's only temporary.

"I'll just put this here for *now* . . ."

By making this statement, most people are trying to convince themselves and others that later, presumably when they're not busy, they will take the misplaced item and triumphantly return it to its proper home (or create a home for it if it's new).

Is this you? Tell us, though. If you were to achieve the ever elusive yet highly coveted state of being "not busy," wouldn't you want to be doing other, more fun things?

The truth is that what you are really saying is, "I have no idea where to put this and am too tired, lazy, flustered, overwhelmed, etc. to find a 'home' for it." *That's where the chaos starts.*

One "for now"? Not terrible, especially if you make it a point to take care of the task within a reasonable time. However, multiple, unresolved "for now's" add up to clutter, and with that clutter comes a loss of control—control over your space and control over your things. Imagine the worst pile of clutter. It's not pretty, and guess what? That pile didn't start out like that. It started with one "for now."

No matter how much time you think you may be saving by avoiding a task or situation "for now," you're only setting yourself up to lose more time later on. Eventually, the pile will get so out of control, you will need hours and hours to go through everything. And you will be very, very aggravated.

So here's what we suggest:

- Keep the "for now's" to a bare minimum, and only when you really can't avoid them.
- Address the ones you can't avoid as soon as you can.
- Take the time to find an easily accessible home for your things and group similar items together, so you minimize the times when you have to say, "I don't have a place for this. I'll just leave it here 'for now.'"
- Finish the task! If you just deal with it now, or as close to now as possible, you will have more time to spend doing the things you love. Yay!

Ok, that's all, folks! We're done. At least *for now*.

"For Later" and "Just-in-Case" Clutter

These two "clutter cousins" both involve holding on to things that you no longer need or use, but for slightly different reasons.

"For Later" clutter is comprised of things you hold on to because you convince yourself you will find another use for them. It could be as simple as a pink ribbon you take off the birthday present you receive in June to save for the breast cancer walk in October, not recalling how much pink ribbon you already have. It might be keeping an excessive number of old plastic supermarket bags to pick up dog poop or line your small trash cans. Or receiving packages and keeping the shipping boxes to use during the holiday season when it's only April.

Now before you get the wrong idea . . . we are big fans of repurposing, not being wasteful, and really being conscious of the environment. We actually recommend it! But there needs to be a limit to how much you keep if you want to stay in control of your space.

"Just-in-Case" clutter is made up of things you don't use anymore and have no current need for, but you save because "you never know when you might need it." In essence, you keep these items *just in case*. This could be anything from old emails and computer files to physical gadgets. One of our clients replaced all her old kitchen appliances but refused to give them away just in case the new ones stopped working! She was taking up a lot of precious space in her garage with things she wasn't even using.

The truth is if you haven't used it in years, you don't need it. Even if a situation were to arise where it would come in handy, it's not worth the space that it is taking up *now* and has been for years. If it doesn't serve your needs, let it go.

Here's the thing: *neither of these categories is clutter unless they take space away from more needed and more often-used items.* If you have enough space to house an excess of "For Later" and "Just-in-Case" stuff and you still have enough space for everything else—all the better!

Marie's husband, Freddie, is a prime example of someone who could potentially have "For Later" clutter. He is commonly referred to as Mr. Fix-it among his immediate family since he is very handy. He is also resourceful. This often means taking something Marie has actually thrown out and storing it in his garage or workroom to repurpose at a later time. He has held on to worn-out, frayed dish towels with holes in them to use when changing the oil in the family cars or varnishing wood moldings. He saves everyone's old toothbrushes to clean parts of machinery that he's fixing or to use when detailing everyone's cars. One of Marie's favorite examples is him wanting old wire hangers so he can clean out narrow pipes if clogged.

Marie really can't fault him for keeping these items because he *does* repurpose each and every one. Luckily, Freddie is mindful about recognizing the space constraints he has in his work area and limits how many "For Later" items he keeps accordingly. (Not to mention it helps to have a wife as a professional organizer who keeps him on point.)

In their case, the "For Later *items*" never become "For Later *clutter*." But for many households, housing this stuff comes at a cost.

Time and space are the main factors you should consider when deciding whether to keep something to use later. Sure, you may be able to repurpose something, but can you afford the space to house it? If you don't give yourself a limit on space, then the items will simply accumulate and begin to take up precious space that could be used for other, more needed items. Annmarie is someone who uses old supermarket bags for dog poop, but she only keeps what will fit in a small basket she has in her closet. She doesn't exceed that space. More on managing space and inventory later in the book.

Similarly, give yourself a timeframe for things you are saving "just in case." If too much time goes by, you might forget you have "temporarily" kept the item and then it will just sit there in the back of the closet or on a shelf in the garage—out of sight and out of mind. In the case of our client who held on to old kitchen appliances, it would have been fine to allow a short timeframe to test out the new ones before relinquishing the old ones. Instead, the old appliances were just forgotten about.

"But There's Nothing Wrong With It" and "I Paid Good Money For It" Clutter

These are things that you are not using, don't like, don't fit into, etc., but you keep them because there's technically nothing wrong with them. They are still in good condition. They still work. You paid a lot of money for them. You tell yourself that maybe you'll sell them, but year after year, they are still sitting in your closet.

The "I Paid Good Money For It" factor can be especially powerful. The negative emotions that accompany buyer's remorse often win out against the logic of letting go of an item they are no longer using. Accordingly, people will keep the expensive item rather than acknowledge a bad purchase. Economist Richard Thaler offers an interesting example of what might happen when you buy a pair of shoes that turn out to be really uncomfortable. Thaler suggests that the more expensive they were, the more often you'll try to wear them in the hopes of breaking them in. If that doesn't work, eventually you'll stop wearing them, but you won't get rid of them. The more you paid for them, the longer they'll sit in the back of your closet. At some point, after the shoes have been fully "depreciated" psychologically, you will finally discard them.[11]

What item(s) do you have depreciating in your closet or drawers?

We get it. It's much easier to give something away or throw something out when it's broken or didn't cost much. But right now, it's costing you space, and it has no value if you're not using, wearing, or selling it.

And like "For Later" and "Just-in-Case" clutter, it's taking up space that's needed for other things.

Aspirational Clutter
This is the clutter that builds up from activities you 1) hoped to do but never did, or 2) supposedly will do in the future "when things settle down." Examples: the hobby or sport you thought you'd try, so you bought every possible accessory and piece of

equipment imaginable but then never really got into it; the cooking magazine you subscribed to when you don't even cook; the videos you purchased because you were finally going to learn French, but never watch. You are keeping all of this because you invested in it and really want to believe that at some point, you will have the time to pursue it.

All this stuff takes up space and causes stress (and is a waste of money if you don't use it!). If you want to try a new hobby, dabble in it for at least a month or two before investing all out. Then you'll know it's something you truly want to make a part of your schedule and your life (and take up space in your home!)

As for stuff you've already gathered? Either commit to your former aspirations and goals and make them a priority, or admit that they are not going to happen and let the stuff go. Aspirations are wonderful. Aspirational clutter is not.

To-Do Clutter

This is the physical documentation related to everyday to-do's: party/event invitations, printed schedules (sports practices & games, fitness classes, etc.), school forms to fill out and return. This paperwork will easily become clutter unless you create an effective system to handle it. Even simple tasks such as creating appointments or accepting party/event invitations will feel like chores if not documented effectively in some sort of planner. And by planner, we don't mean a gazillion sticky notes placed on the fridge or counter to remind us to make a dentist appointment or call a friend on her birthday. Sticky notes = clutter unless used very specifically.

When you decide something is a "to do," write it down in a physical planner or planning app. This is your list, or "tickler," to remind you of what needs to be done. The physical papers associated with the "to-do" list should be gathered in a "to-do" folder, so there is one place to find them when you need them.

Then your number one "to do" should be making an appointment with yourself! Block out time to tackle house chores, exercise, go shopping, or make important calls. At the start of this designated time, go to your physical "to-do" folder and work your way through your list. As you become more used to this process, focus on prioritizing your tasks—by due date, importance, or "I'll be in the area anyway and can get this done."

Successful people work smarter, not harder. They make it look easy because they are scheduling their time well, and honoring the appointments they make with themselves to get through their to-do lists in a timely way.

Mental Clutter

As we mentioned earlier, mental clutter is in a class all by itself. It isn't tangible, so it's often overlooked in terms of its classification as a type of clutter. But it packs a big punch and causes havoc on a lot of levels.

We are inundated in today's world with the never ending pace of communication. With so much technology around us, we are technically reachable 24/7. It's not like the good ol' days when the only interruption might be a phone call where you could let the answering machine pick up. Now we get interrupted by constant alerts and notifications for texts, social media posts, and emails. Our mind is then filled with thoughts of who it might be and what it might be about, and what we lose is focus on the task at hand. What a threat to productivity!

Another example of mental clutter relates to To-Do clutter: when you try to keep appointments, dates, activities and to-dos all in your head. It's hard to stay present when you are focused on all the things you have to do. This is especially true when you don't use a planner, notebook or smartphone app to assist you in managing it all.

Then there are thoughts that don't serve us, such as negative self-talk ("I'm not good enough," "I'll never be organized," "I don't have what it takes.") and defeatist statements such as "I can't."

Mental clutter is relevant because it depletes us of energy, making it difficult to focus on more productive and solution-focused thinking. It can also lead to anxiety and depression, and prevent us from moving forward.

We are not medical professionals and aren't qualified to assist you in treating any clinical diagnoses associated with mental clutter (such as anxiety and depression). However, we are qualified to teach you strategies to help manage your time, space, belongings, and energy. We hope that in doing so, we will help you create an upward spiral, and that our work together will be one path towards making positive and empowering changes in your life.

Who's ready for a clutter detox?

Detoxing is not just good for the body, it's good for your home, too. All that clutter is like a poison—the more it builds up, the quicker it tears you down in one way, shape, or form. The organizing process is like a good detox—it gets rid of the toxins (clutter) so the body (your home/office/space) can run more efficiently. Like a real detox, the process requires serious commitment to changing old behaviors, but when it's done you will feel amazing and have so much positive energy!

Understanding how clutter shows up in our lives is an important first step in the process of eliminating it. In the next section, we introduce our Top Eight Organizing Principles. They are designed to help you avoid clutter and create organizing systems to save you time, money, space and energy.

Let's get started!

PART II

THE EIGHT PRINCIPLES

CHAPTER 4

Goal Setting and Other Tools for Your Organizing Toolbox

In the introduction, we spoke about hope being the foundation for all change. On some level, you simply must believe that things can change in order for them to actually do so. You must also believe in your ability to find pathways to achieving your desired goals. Otherwise, there would be no motivating force to keep you going.

If you truly believed that nothing you do would make a difference, why would you even try? Our sense of hope is largely tied to our goals and our thought processes on how to attain them.[12] Hope is what gives us motivation. Motivation is what keeps us going when we encounter challenges and obstacles. And let's face it, there will always be challenges and obstacles.

Since you are reading this book, we will happily assume this means you've chosen it as one pathway to your goal of becoming more organized! First of all, yay! Second of all, this brings us to an important point: what does it mean to you to "become more organized"?

The problem with this phrase is that it is vague, not to mention subjective. This same statement will mean very different things to different people. So it's imperative that you gain clarity on what it is you wish to accomplish.

Does "becoming more organized" mean:

- Getting better at time management?
  I never show up on time. My friends are angry with me because I say I'll be ready and then never am. I'm late for meetings at work and miss deadlines. My team doesn't respect me as a leader and my superiors pass me up for promotions. I feel that there aren't enough hours in the day for me to balance my work life with family life.

- Decluttering your home so you can feel happy and confident having guests over?
  I want to invite friends and family over, but I'm embarrassed for them to see how I am living. They think I have it all together; I can't bear the thought of them finding out the truth. Or . . . There's nowhere for us to sit and my kitchen is so cluttered, how could I possibly entertain? My counters are such a mess.

- Purging through your clothing and eliminating what you are no longer using because it no longer fits, is stained or is out-of-style?

*I can't fit the stuff I **am** using because my closets, drawers and shelves are filled with things I never use. I hate that I can never find anything to wear. A lot of times I replace something, only to find that I had it all along. There are a lot of clothes I would wear, but since I can't see them, I forget I even have them.*

- Developing a system for managing your paperwork (incoming mail, school papers, kids' artwork)?
  I am drowning in paper. So much mail comes every day and I don't know what to do with it. I'm not paying my bills on time because I don't know which one is due when. I have so many magazines, I could start my own store, but I still want to read them all because I paid for the subscriptions. My kids' paperwork and projects are out of control. I don't know what to keep and what not to. How can I throw any of it out . . . they will think I don't love them!

These are just a few examples of clearer objectives. Once you establish what yours are, you can then set related goals and establish an action plan accordingly. When you begin to think through a goal, you should be motivated by the thought of achieving it for *you*, not your husband/mother/friend/etc. We're most likely to achieve goals that align with our values and motivate us.[13]

Often people avoid the organizing process because they just feel completely overwhelmed by the enormity of the task ahead of them. The project seems so massive and unattainable that they feel defeated and exhausted before they even begin. The key is to break it down into smaller, more realistic and—this is important—*attainable*—goals. Think of organizing as one giant game of Pac-Man. Pac-Man doesn't finish the board in one shot; he tackles it one bite at a time. The successful organizer approaches life the same way. Pac-Man destroys his enemies by eating the flashing power pellets. Our power pellets are our tried-and-true principles—"Finishing the Task," "Grouping Like with Like," "Everything Deserves a Home," etc. There will be setbacks and times when you lose your focus. But with perseverance and trying different routes, you—like the Pacster—will achieve success and move to the next level. Each success will motivate and inspire you to keep going, and soon you will go from out of control to organizing guru!

Setting SMART goals

If you are new to goal setting, we recommend starting with the SMART system.[14]

Over time, the definition of the acronym has changed to meet the needs of the person or organization using it. For our purposes, we suggest that each of your goals meet all of the following criteria:

S—Specific
M—Measurable
A—Attainable

R—Realistic

T—Timely

Let's break it down to make it really easy to understand:

Specific

Your goal should be well-defined and clear. As we mentioned earlier, "I want to get more organized." is vague. A clearer goal would be, "I want to establish a simple system for paying my bills."

Measurable

There should be some way to indicate that your goal has been met. This might be some type of quantifiable measure, or any type of evidence that you have achieved what you originally set out to do. In the example above, it might mean paying bills on time for a set number of months without incurring late fees.

Attainable and realistic

The goals you set should be challenging but possible given factors such as your skillset, available time, other current priorities, financial means, and access to required resources. If you are an accountant during tax season and are also a caregiver to an ailing parent, you may not have the time available to embark on a full-scale paper management project. In this case, you might wish to establish smaller-scale goals that involve a single element of the process—such as opening your mail every day.

Timely

Rather than keeping a goal open-ended, set a date for completion. This will help keep you motivated and will influence how you manage your to-do list in relation to your goal. You don't want to get sidetracked by everyday tasks that arise, but rather stay focused on what is truly the priority for the day. You should be realistic when setting a deadline; it should give you enough time to achieve the goal, but still be soon enough to keep you motivated.

For our paper-management example, the simple task of opening mail every day is a critical first step. Note: If you are someone for whom paperwork is not an issue, this advice may seem ridiculously simplistic. However, for the person who struggles, this "simple" task is anything but simple. In fact, it is a necessary habit to establish in order to ensure success.

If you've set a goal of creating a simple system and have given yourself two months to have it up and running successfully, then you will be more intentional about putting "open mail" as a daily priority on your to-do list. Without the deadline, it's easier to say, "All these unexpected things came up. My child has a project. My boss gave me extra work. I have so much laundry. I'll open the mail tomorrow."

The SMART system has been around for decades because it works, and yet it is just one of many tools to keep in your organizing toolbox. Here are a few others to take your goals from SMART to BEYOND SMART:

Put your goals in writing

According to a research study on goal setting conducted by psychology professor Dr. Gail Matthews at the Dominican University in California, you are 42 percent more likely to achieve your goals if you write them down. Forty-two percent![15]

In terms of your organizing goals, it can be as simple as writing or typing out a sentence: "I, [Your Name], commit to sticking to my new paper management system" and—this is important—*hanging it where you can see it.*

Sound silly? If you don't believe us, listen to Olympic Gold Medalist Michael Phelps:

"I write my goals down on a piece of paper and they're there where I can see them because I have to have a reason, I have to see something for why I'm getting up in the morning and what I'm doing that day."[16]

You could also declare it on social media, if you so dare. Nothing like putting a goal online for your 1,200+ "friends" to see to get the ball rolling! A girl we know was so determined to reach her goal of sticking to her new fitness routine that she scheduled a bikini photoshoot on the beach for a few months later. She vowed that she would go through with it no matter how she looked and would post the pictures publicly on her Facebook page.

The end result? A kick ass photoshoot showing amazing fitness results! Not sure if it was motivation or just plain terror, but it worked. She put it out there publicly and in writing. By doing so, it psychologically upped her commitment to staying consistent and keeping her promise to herself (and her 1,200+ online friends).

There are varying viewpoints on whether or not making a goal public increases the odds of success in goal setting. We are firm believers in *doing what works for you*. Sometimes, that simply means trying different approaches until you find what makes you tick. When you do, this self-awareness will serve you as you move forward on other goals.

Plan to fail

You may be thinking, "Um, not very motivating, ladies . . ." It's not that we don't believe in you! It's just inevitable that things will "come up" that may throw you off track (and by "you" we mean anyone who is striving to achieve a goal, including us!).

We have a friend who is constantly starting a diet. She buys the trending book, joins social media groups, stocks her fridge with whatever she needs and launches full force into it. *She always starts strong.* As long as everything else in her world stays constant, she does very well. The minute something unexpected happens, however, she is thrown off course. And most of the time, she doesn't recover and she gives up. It makes her feel terrible and launches her into a downward spiral of negativity. ("Why bother? I just can't do it.")

Although we may have gotten your attention with the word "fail," what we really want to talk about is the importance of thinking about possible pitfalls or obstacles to reaching your goals. This is one of those times when thinking about the past can be really beneficial.

- "What happened in the past that caused me to derail off course or quit?"
- "What tested my willpower the most?"
- "Why was it difficult to bounce back quickly?"

In addition, it's important to think about the goal in terms of your current situation, reality, resources, schedule and other factors:

- "What could go wrong?"
- "What might get in the way of my goal?"
- "What is challenging about my schedule or responsibilities that might keep me from doing what I need to do?"

Once you have made a list of possible pitfalls, you can then establish "implementation intentions" to use in response if necessary. Implementation intentions are self-driven behaviors written in "if X, then Y" format. More specifically, "If X situation arises, then I will perform Y behavior in response."[17] They can be used to reduce stress and keep you on course in the event that you encounter the unexpected. Essentially, you are creating your Plan B.

Let's stick with our paper example: You've established a set date to pay your bills, but today the school nurse calls and says your young child is sick and needs to be picked up. You know once you get home, your baby will want and need all your attention. Of course that takes precedence over the bills! With an implementation intention, you already have a plan for just this type of situation. "If something prevents me from paying the bills today, then I will wake up an hour earlier tomorrow and do it then" *or* "I will take them to work tomorrow and take care of it during my lunch hour."

Having this strategy in place helps you in a few ways:

- There's no guesswork, and therefore less stress. There's no negativity, because you will feel more in control knowing that this unexpected turn of events won't throw you off the path to achieving your organizing goals.

- You don't need to expend any mental or physical energy figuring out how you are going to handle things. You've prepared in advance, so you won't be losing any willpower. Willpower is necessary for staying on target.[18]

Establish "primers"

Simply put, primers (also known as "primes") are cues or reminders that trigger a call to action for your goals. Examples of primers include: a screen saver with a motivating quote; a reminder alarm; a to-do list; vision boards; ring tones, etc.

When the situation fits, we encourage clients to associate the task they want to accomplish with another family member's task. For example, when the kids sit down to do homework, we might encourage the parent to do his or her "homework," i.e., pay the bills, at the same time. The primer is the kids sitting to do their homework.

Michael Phelps' written goal is his primer. As you can see from his quote on page 47, not only does he make it visible, but he also puts it in a place where it's the first thing he sees. The primer sets the tone for the day and how he approaches it.

What's a primer you can use to help you reach your goal?

Accountability

Being accountable to someone other than yourself can be a huge asset in reaching your goals. The key is to find someone to report your progress to who cares about your success. It could be a family member, friend, co-worker, coach, or therapist— anyone whom you trust to keep track of how well you are doing. It should also be someone who is ready to root for you and be your cheerleader. You want someone who is eager to celebrate and savor your wins, but is a safe harbor for you when you hit obstacles or make mistakes. Let them know what you are looking to accomplish, when you wish to accomplish it, and how you will let them know.

In our example, you might text your best friend at the end of each month and let her know that you paid your bills on time without incurring late fees.

Another great way to be accountable is to find an accountability partner—someone who is also looking to achieve new organizing goals. You can set goals together, help each other with organizing projects, and keep each other focused and motivated. Fun Fact: Becoming "unofficial" accountability partners is how the idea for our business was born!

Here's an excerpt from the "Our Story" page on our website. At the time we didn't realize we were acting as accountability partners (we were just trying not to lose our minds!). But looking back, that's exactly what we became and it served us well on a lot of levels!

When we were deciding what we wanted to be when we grew up, the term "professional organizer" didn't come to mind, quite frankly because it didn't exist! We both attained business degrees in college and went on to pursue careers in sales and marketing.

Annmarie worked in advertising sales and production for four trade magazines before being hired as an account executive for a pharmaceutical advertising agency. She then worked for several years as a project manager for a successful qualitative market research firm. In all three positions, Annmarie relied heavily upon her organizational skills, as well as her ability to handle direct client contact and meet almost impossibly tight deadlines.

Marie worked for years as a senior account sales representative for a major office products corporation before being promoted to sales manager. Excellent time and territory management skills were critical to her success in consistently attaining her extensive sales goals. From there, she was hired as director of sales/marketing for a nationally known relief organization. Her organizational skills were essential in managing her staff and handling the significant workload for which her department was responsible.

We were on top of our game and doing just fine and then [cue: screeching halt sound effect]: We had kids.

Suddenly, we were home all day trying to keep little humans alive. As much as we had managed a great deal of responsibility before, this was on a whole other level!

Despite the fact that we had strong organizational skills, this was a major life event that affected our day-to-day priorities and activities in a significant way. It took time to figure out and navigate this "new normal." Our to-do lists were completely different, and so were our priorities. We were operating on a different timeframe, one often dictated by the schedule and needs of our children.

We had to adapt, reset our way of thinking, and restore the balance. We did, but it didn't happen overnight. And it took a lot of trial and error.

The good thing is we were two friends going through a similar upheaval at the same time. So we started brainstorming and sharing ideas. We tried different things and slowly figured out how to balance our schedules and to-dos and the enormous responsibility that goes along with raising little ones. And then we started helping our friends. So much so that we started to hear, "You should do this for a living!" and "There's so many of us out there that could benefit from your ideas!"

Another great thing was that this was during a time when all these organizing shows were popping up on TV: "Clean Sweep," "Clean House," "Neat." HGTV was getting hugely popular, and people were more familiar with the idea of home and self-improvement. So we actually started kicking around the idea. Could it work? Would people actually pay us to teach them how to be organized? We talked and talked about it for over a year but did nothing about it. Then one day a dear friend who owned her own design business called and said she had a client that needed us. She said, "You're going there on Tuesday." We said, "What? We don't have a company, we don't have a name, we don't even have a flyer." She patiently but firmly replied, "You're going." So we did, and a second career was born.

The change process can be difficult. It's so much more fun when you have someone to go through it with! Think of it like having a workout partner.

Who could you ask to either hold you accountable or be your accountability partner in (organizing) crime? Why did you choose this person or persons?

And last but not least . . .

Celebrate the wins!

This is a *big* one for us! We are strong supporters of the notion that even small progress is progress. Anything you accomplish that moves you forward, however small, should be celebrated. We don't want you focusing on what you didn't get done and feeling bad about it. We want you recognizing what you *did* complete and feeling *great* about it!

Each success will motivate you to keep going and also increase your feeling of self-efficacy, which is also something to celebrate!

Why this principle is important

Setting SMART goals and having a plethora of tools in your organizing toolbox allows you to:

- Create a more effective action plan for reaching your goals.
- Better prioritize your to-dos and action steps.
- Immediately adjust when obstacles arise without stress.
- Stay focused and motivated throughout the process.
- Increase your chances of success.
- Increase your sense of self-efficacy.

What mastering this principle will save you

Time: The clearer the goal, the more effective the action plan and the quicker the results. People who don't have clear goals often spend a lot of time working on to-dos without making progress. We find they don't prioritize as well, even when they are seemingly checking a lot of items off their to-do list daily.

Money: BEYOND SMART goals lead to success, which will *always* save you money in the long run. You may save in late fees because you are paying your bills on time. You may save money by not replacing things you already own because you have good systems in place. You may find valuable items and actual money in the decluttering process. Fun Fact: We have found (and surprised our clients with) thousands of dollars in cash and missing jewelry over the years. *Thousands.*

Energy: Behavior change takes commitment, work, and focus, which means it takes energy! How clear and prepared you are will determine how much extra energy you spend during the process. Having an implementation intention saves a lot of energy because you don't even have to *think* about a Plan B— it's already established and ready to go!

Space: If your goal involves decluttering, you will definitely save space (or at least use it more effectively!). No matter what the goal, however, you will also clear space in your mind for other things you wish to focus on.

CHAPTER 5

Have a Vision for Each Space and Establish Clear Zones

In the last chapter, we spoke about setting BEYOND SMART goals and really getting clear on what you personally mean when you say you wish to get organized. When it comes to decluttering projects, that clarity comes into play once more.

Whenever we approach a new project, we always ask our clients, "What is your vision for this space?" We need to understand what purpose the room or area needs to serve, in essence, what it needs to "be." Defining that purpose is important because it focuses the mind and behavior towards a specific end result. The clearer your vision, the more intentional and "on target" your decision making will be. You will be approaching each decision with that vision in mind, rather than just making random choices.

This would be much easier if every space or room could be its own thing: a bedroom for sleeping and relaxing; a kitchen for cooking and eating; even a coat closet for just, well, coats! And maybe some accessories, too.

However, often a space isn't just "one thing." For example, a basement may need to be a family room, home office, and home gym all at the same time. We don't always have the luxury of designing a space for a single purpose.

Similarly, even when a room serves a single function (e.g., storage), it may need to house several different categories. Although they may need to "live together," these categories may not have anything to do with each other (or belong to the same family member!).

When a room needs to serve multiple purposes—in function and/or in category—it's essential to create clear zones. For example, we organized a garage for a client who used it to store holiday decorations, sports equipment (for 5 kids!), pantry items, tools, and more. When we arrived, all of these categories were mixed together. By separating things out and assigning a particular section of the space to each category, the garage became much more efficient and a real asset to this busy household.

It's only when you have a clear vision that you can determine how much space to allocate for each section or zone. Also, it will help you to identify more easily which items need to remain in the space and which ones need to go elsewhere. More about that in the chapter on deciding what stays and what goes. For the moment, let's stay focused on the space itself.

How can you create this vision?

Some people are really great at seeing beyond what is physically in front of them and imagining what *could be*. Others need more help in this regard. Have you ever watched home improvement shows on channels like HGTV? It's incredible to witness designers, architects, and contractors working together to totally transform a home. They seem to have bionic eyes that penetrate through the clutter and previous design to imagine a different layout, color scheme, and decor.

Although you may not be doing a major renovation or knocking down walls, there are ways to tap into your inner designer/architect. Even if this is not your usual modus operandi, we fully encourage you to activate your growth mindset and get curious about what's possible.

What do you envision this room to look like?

Remember in the introduction when we begged you to stop looking at Pinterest? That's because too many people see these perfect looking organizing pictures and set unrealistic goals for themselves. However, Pinterest is a great tool when used for visioning. And don't worry if you aren't tech savvy or prefer "old school" approaches. This project can be done just as easily with good old fashioned magazines, scissors, glue, and paper.

Start out in a more general way by looking at organizing pictures that appeal to you. If you're already on Pinterest, great! Create a vision board for this project. If not, a simple Internet search will do the trick and you can always save photos to a folder on your desktop. As you gather photos on your board or in your folder, see if patterns emerge regarding what appeals to you. Do you like clear surfaces or pictures with visible organizing products? Are you drawn to open spaces? Do you prefer lighter color schemes? Solids vs. patterns?

Take note of any emotions that come up when you look at various pictures. Which ones make you feel calm and capable? Which bring up feelings of anxiety or being out of control? Try to hone in on what the triggers are, both positive and negative. This can be very eye-opening, since we often adapt to the way we've been living and aren't conscious of things that may be causing us stress. It may be as simple as the difference between using a solid color tablecloth or a busy patterned one. When the kitchen table needs to be your desk, that busy tablecloth might be a serious detriment to your productivity because it could make it difficult to focus on the work in front of you. In contrast, a plain solid tablecloth might act as a blank slate and evoke a calmer feeling.

If you like to work more in list form, you can make one using characteristics you'd like the room to have, such as "uncluttered," "good flow," and "lots of storage."

Now ask yourself these questions in terms of your specific space:

- What is the goal of this room/space? Will it serve more than one function?

- Is the space big enough for the amount of things going in it? That is, is it feasible for it to serve that many functions and accommodate the amount of furniture and items that it will need to?

- Which family members will be using or have access to this room?

- What is the visibility of the room/space? For example, is it on the main floor? Will it be used for entertaining or just be seen by you?

- Is there any furniture/decor currently in this room that can be discarded? If so, what is it?

- Is there any furniture/decor in this room that *must* stay? If so, what is it and why (budget/sentimentality/super functional/your spouse will leave you if you get rid of it)?

Getting both a general and more specific vision of your likes and dislikes will help you make the best use of your space when you are ready to start. Also, when you factor in the other people who will be using the space, you will make smarter choices about which factors are non-negotiable and which require compromise.

When organizing multi-purpose rooms, we highly recommend having a family meeting to get input from the others who will be using the space. Involving them in both the conversation and the process will give them a better understanding of what you are trying to create. It will also help increase their "buy-in." The stronger their buy-in, the stronger their effort will be to maintain organization. You will all be working to achieve a common goal: to have a wonderful, functional, and uncluttered space.

Once everyone is on the same page with what the vision for the room is and how many functions it needs to serve, you can start by literally mapping out the room. The layout of a room can determine whether or not it will set your family up to succeed or fail when it comes to keeping things organized.

The fun challenge here is achieving balance between creating the necessary zones and yet still having a "flow" to the room. If the room will be multi-functional, does one function take priority over the others (e.g., the primary breadwinner's home office vs. the home gym)? Is there one that affects more family members than others (e.g. the playroom vs. long-term filing)? This might affect where that zone is planned on "The Map."

If the room is not multi-functional per se, but rather needs to store multiple categories, decide which items need to be the most accessible. Or figure out which categories will be accessed by the most family members, since this will mean the most traffic! When mapping out the room, consider placing these items closer to the entrance. The ultimate goal is to make it as easy as possible for your loved ones to find what they need *and* to put it back when they are done! Sometimes, the less they have to travel the better.

Other things to consider: What does the room already have going for it? Are there closets to use for storage? Do you have appropriate shelving? Do you have *any* shelving? Look at your vertical wall space and not just the floor plan. Well used vertical space can be a game changer! See the bonus section at the end of the chapter for more on ideas on how to maximize yours.

These things may also be the deciding factor in where the different zones should be. For example, in Annmarie's basement, they set up the office near the closet in the back with a shelving unit, so it could be used for office supplies. Their home gym area was set up in a space where the treadmill could fit and still face the TV, and coincidentally next to closets with mirrored doors. The mirrors work well for maintaining proper form while working out, so it was a win-win!

When mapping out the zones, think about the furniture or storage pieces that are already there. Will they work with what you are trying to accomplish? Before buying anything new, think about furniture you may not be using effectively in other rooms and see if it will work in this space.

One of our clients didn't want to part with a dresser that had belonged to her deceased grandmother. At the same time, it didn't match her décor at all and was sitting unused and collecting dust in her attic. This did not honor her grandmother and the piece took space away from other things our client was using. When we organized her attic space, she wanted it to be a playroom for her children, a place to watch movies as a family and a storage space for luggage, seasonal clothes, and extra household supplies. It was also where she kept all her gift wrapping supplies. We encouraged her to think outside the box and consider how her grandmother's dresser could be incorporated into the design or function of the space. In the end, she came up with the idea to use it as a gift wrapping station. The drawers now hold bows, ribbon, wrapping paper, gift bags, tissue paper and cards, as well as scissors and tape. Every time our client wraps a gift, she has everything she needs at her fingertips and remembers her grandmother with a smile. When she savors those positive feelings and memories, she is also increasing her well-being.

If you do eventually buy a new piece, don't buy simply for design; consider functionality and storage capacity as well. Marie used to get, shall we say . . . frustrated, with her husband Freddie when he would come home from work and dump out his pockets on the granite counter in her kitchen. He would hang up his coat and walk through the living room in order to do this. This was bad enough. Freddie started his career as a mechanical engineer and used to work in the field every day. His pockets became storage for everything, including his wedding ring when he occasionally took it off at work! (Yes, we know, but that's a whole other chapter!) At one point, he couldn't find his wedding ring for about three months. Turns out it got mixed in with a bunch of loose change the kids were collecting in an old coffee can. They had raided Freddie's "dump pile" on the kitchen counter and didn't realize the ring was among the coins. They only found it because one day, Marie and the kids rolled up the coins in paper wrappers so they could bring them to the bank. Lo and behold, there in the can it was!

So when Marie was buying a table for her entryway, she bought a piece with drawers so that Freddie could have a place to put all his pocket clutter. Now he has a designated place for his stuff (conveniently located right where the coats are hung up) and she no longer has to deal with it being in the kitchen. The piece also has a cabinet underneath with shelving that she uses to store photo albums that were not easily accessible in the past. In this age of digital pictures where memories are sometimes lost in the abyss, she really enjoys looking through the albums with her family. She could have easily bought something just based on its looks. Instead, she maximized storage by remembering her vision for the space—an uncluttered entryway to her living room where the family could relax and spend quality time together. She also kept the peace with her hubby and created an opportunity to bond with the family and savor happy memories. *This is a beautiful example of how conscious, intentional planning and organization enriches lives beyond what can be seen on the surface.*

Now while we do encourage you to plan and think things through, we don't want you to get stuck either. If you don't have furniture to repurpose, are on a limited budget, or need a little time to shop around, don't let that stop you from starting your project. You don't have to spend a lot to maximize space in a room. Heck, we can organize you with shoe boxes if necessary! Simply using repurposed items from your home or just buying a few essentials like bins or cardboard storage boxes can be enough temporarily. Nowadays there are a lot of inexpensive options that look great and hold up well over time.

This brings us to an important point about this principle: just because we are encouraging you to spend time creating a vision for the space, we do not expect you to have all the answers once you are done. The benefit of this principle is to get you to a place where you are in tune with your needs, wishes, and hopes for the space. *Our goal is to help you increase your self-awareness.* We want you to be more intentional with how you approach the process and consequently, the decisions you make throughout. That is why this is such an important step, albeit one that is often skipped over.

Furthermore, some people buy organizing products (and even big-ticket furniture items) and then design their vision around them. Doing it this way can actually *cost* you more time and money, as well as reduce your options because you are limited to the pieces you've invested in. If you vision first, your mindset will be broader and more open, and your eyes will actually "see" more possibilities. That's not to say you shouldn't use items you already have, or that you won't decide to buy the exact same pieces in the end. But by visioning first and buying second, you are making a more thoughtful and informed decision.

Organizing is trial and error, so even after you've worked on the space, "living with it" for a few weeks or a month will help you decide if you made all the right choices for you and your family. Not all successes happen on the first try. In addition to building awareness by visioning, you will also learn a lot about yourself and your family in the actual use of the organized space, and tweak the organizing accordingly. You may decide that you need a different type of system or product. You might wish to change the flow of the room. The point is, this principle is about doing some inner work first in order to create the best physical reflection of that work. Deep, huh? It really is. Be patient.

Other ways to apply this principle

Although we have been using an entire room as an example, this principle can be applied to any space or project, including closets and things like binders or file systems.

For a closet, visualizing what the space needs to house will help you make better decisions regarding where everything should go and which organizers should be used. You will be able to think through what needs to be easily accessible versus what will not be accessed very often but still needs to be stored. Having clear zones—in this case, categories—will help you manage your inventory better and prevent overbuying (more on that in chapter 10).

For a binder, keeping categories separate within it will help you keep track of paperwork and prevent important papers from being lost. A great example of this is the "College Prep Binder"[19] Marie created for each of her children when they were preparing to submit their applications. They had to keep track of multiple types of paperwork, including test scores, important dates, application requirements, and financial information. Each category was its own labeled section in the binder. Marie's husband Freddie handled the financial end of the process. By having a separate section for that paperwork, Freddie was easily able to find what he needed at any given moment *and* he had no reason to mess up the paperwork that didn't apply to him. Marie's children also were able to take a more independent and proactive role in the process—and as a result, their future—without having to ask Mom for every little thing they needed to complete their applications. Proud to say they are both thriving in college!

Why this principle is important

Having a clear vision will help you:

- Increase self-awareness on how a room's design and layout impact your mood and overall well-being.
- Create a more efficient and aesthetically pleasing layout.
- Allocate your space effectively.
- Design a space that will set you up for organizing success.
- Make more focused and rational decisions about what should be kept in the room, instead of random, more

emotional ones that don't support the vision and goal for the space.

Establishing clear zones:

- Makes it easier to find what you need and to put it away.
- Decreases the likelihood of the space becoming a dumping ground.
- Gives you more control over your space and reduces stress and anxiety.

What mastering this principle will save you

Time: You will save time in the organizing process itself, because your decision making will be more intentional. You will make quicker decisions because they will be based upon whether or not the item supports the vision for the space. With clear zones, you won't waste time looking for something in an area of the room where it shouldn't be. You will know exactly where to go and where to look, and bypass the rest of the space. You will also save time in the long run because having clear zones means that things can be easily returned to where they belong, meaning less time spent having to re-organize all over again.

Money: Mindfully exploring options for repurposing furniture and items you already own and/or reimagining vertical wall space will prevent the need to spend more than is necessary. If you do make purchases, they will be with a specific design and purpose in mind. Random purchases always = higher spending without guaranteeing a good return on investment. Being able to find what you need more easily in your clearly defined zones means less replacing of items you already own.

Energy: Visualizing your ideal space—taking note of what evokes feelings of peace, tranquility, calm, and control—will put you in a more positive state of mind. Your decision making will be less stressful and therefore you will expend a lot less energy. You will not get depleted as quickly and therefore you will have better emotional regulation and more energy for other endeavors. Having clear zones means less running around within the space when you are looking for something or attempting to put it away.

Space: While this principle doesn't necessarily save you space, it helps you maximize and make better use of it. And in some cases, you will gain space you weren't previously using, such as vertical (wall) space.

Bonus: Working with vertical space

Too many times people only look at the square footage of a room and what usable floor space they have. They mistakenly think that's all there is to work with. We encourage you to think outside the box (or in this case, the floor!) Look *up* as well as down! Your vertical wall space provides amazing potential for organizing solutions, whether you are handy or not:

- **Shelving:** Instead of putting a picture or mirror above a dresser or storage unit, use that space to install shelves that can house books, decorative bins, binders, etc. If done correctly, these shelves can serve as a functional element as well as a decorative one.
- **Taller storage units:** With or without doors, your upper wall space gives you more choices when it comes to storage pieces. These days, there are so many options for pieces that accommodate smaller spaces, so even areas where you don't have a lot of depth, you can compensate by using its height.
- **Hooks:** These handy dandy treasures are scoring big wins in homes, offices, and dorm rooms alike! Not just for coats anymore, they are great for hanging jewelry, hats, handbags and all sorts of must-keep-accessible items. Hang them on an empty wall or the door to a room or cabinet. And with the dawn of peel and stick hooks, the damage risk has been reduced so low you can experiment to your heart's content!
- **Baker's racks and other open shelving units:** From sturdy plastic to stainless steel, these easy-to-assemble storage giants are great for creating instant storage without the hassle of manually installing shelves (or hiring someone else to do so). For a wonderful example

of how to use wall space effectively using open shelving units, see the case studies at the end of the book.

- **Over-the-door storage organizers:** So many choices, so little time! You can find ones to house jewelry, toiletries, shoes, bags, etc. Essentially what these units are doing is capitalizing on vertical space!

- **Storage bins:** While this is not the most aesthetically pleasing option, it still is a very efficient and viable one for those who may not yet be ready to make a more permanent purchase. Well-made bins that are the same type and size will stack well so you can minimize the amount of floor space you take up for storage. Group your items by category and then stack the bins accordingly.

- **Free-standing mudroom benches:** Why settle for just a bench when you can have cubbies or hooks, too? And why limit them to a mudroom? Some homes (like ours) don't even have mudrooms! These stand-alone units can be used in the entry way of any busy space throughout the house.

What are some of your ideas for maximizing vertical space?

CHAPTER 6

Sort Through Your Belongings and Group "Like with Like"

If we had to hone in on the part of the process that stresses out clients the most, it would have to be the task of sorting through their belongings. Hands down.

Actually, we take that back. What really stresses people out is the idea that they have to *part* with their belongings. We'll cover that in the next chapter.

The sorting process is a close second, though, because the thought of starting can seem so daunting, especially when the pile to sort through is very large. If you're familiar with the Netflix series, "Tidying Up with Marie Kondo," you may have watched (quite possibly in horror) as the featured family is encouraged to empty the entire contents of their drawers and closets into a massive pile to sort through. However, there is a reason Ms. Kondo wants you to do this. She knows that seeing everything you have accumulated in one place will have an impact on your perspective and decision making. It's important to do this if you are going to truly embrace each piece and decide whether or not it brings you joy.

However, we do recognize how overwhelming this might seem when you are working on your own and not with the support of a professional organizer. In fact, one of the most crucial ways we help our clients is by making this very task as easy to handle as possible, while being present and supportive throughout the process.

Therefore, we would like to expand upon this concept and teach you how to make the process more manageable. Rather than create one big pile, we invite you to sort through everything in the space and group like items together, or "like with like." For our purposes, we describe these piles of "like items" as categories. If you are working on your kitchen, for example, your pots and pans could be its own category. This would be fairly clear, as a pot is a pot. A category could also reflect types of items that serve a similar purpose. For example, you might gather batteries, light bulbs, flashlights, and extension cords in a pile and call it "utility." This type of category might be different from home to home, but the categorical idea is the same.

Now this is a good time to remind you, our treasured reader, that not only did we not invent organizing, we didn't invent "grouping like with like" either. You will find that many organizers use this important concept in their work. What we have done is found our own way to explain it, teach it, incorporate it and hopefully, help people with it. (Now back to our regularly scheduled chapter . . .)

We call this "The Helping Principle" because it works hand in hand with most of the others, such as: "Have a Vision/ Establish Clear Zones," "Creating Associations," "Decide What Stays and What Goes," "Everything Deserves a Home," and "Manage Your Space/Inventory." It supports the others and creates a myriad of benefits. However, let's first discuss what it means on its own.

We have found that most people have no idea how much they have because the same type of item can be found all throughout the home. When you gather it all in one place, you can really see just what you have (and how much of it) and then make reasonable, informed choices about what stays and what goes.

We promise that you will make a different decision when you see that you have ten or twenty of the same item versus when you think you only have one or two.

Here's an example we've been using for years (we have no idea why we chose potato peelers. Please just roll with it!):

Say you have six kitchen drawers and you have a potato peeler in each one. It doesn't seem out of the ordinary because every time you open a drawer, you only see one potato peeler. But if you were to empty all the drawers and group "like with like," then you would realize that you have six potato peelers. And that's when you need to ask yourself just how many potatoes you plan on making at one time! How many helpers will you ever have using all those peelers? "Grouping Like with Like" will help you make informed choices about how much you really need and how much space you can save by admitting it.

Having like items grouped together also makes the decision-making process itself much less overwhelming. Even better is when you can further group within the original sorting. For example, whenever we sort through clothes, we don't just separate tops from bottoms. We separate the tops into three sub-piles: "sleeveless," "short sleeve," and "long sleeve." If we're dealing with, say, sweatshirts, we'll separate pullovers from zip-ups, and hoodies from non-hoodies, etc. We take a similar approach with bottoms (long pants, capris, shorts, skorts) and dresses (by sleeve or skirt length, evening versus casual, etc.).

Then we remove our client from the room where all the sorting has been done and *give them one category at a time to purge through*. In doing so, they are able to focus on just that one pile *without getting overwhelmed by the rest of it*. They are not distracted and can better think through the reasons for keeping, discarding, or donating their things. Additionally, when a task is overwhelming, it is also very draining. Removing some of the stress helps keep their energy up, giving them more stamina throughout the process.

Now, in our clothing example, these sorts are deliberate; we look for these categories. With other projects, we just start sorting and the categories emerge. This is often the case with garages and basements, although it can happen in any space where multiple categories are mixed together. We'll find categories such as utility items (lightbulbs, batteries, tools, filters, etc.), sports equipment, holiday decorations, electronics, among others.

Once the sorting process is done, the challenge is making sure that the categories you've found *don't also reside in other areas of the home*. For example, are there batteries in multiple drawers and closets? If so, we encourage you to group them all together so you can keep track of what you have.

Let's consider how a supermarket is stocked. All the cold items are in the dairy and freezer aisles. Within each aisle, however, specific types of foods are grouped together (yogurt, cheese, frozen veggies, ice cream) to make it easier for the consumer to shop. All the pet food is in one aisle while the cleaning products are in a different aisle (or clearly delineated in a different section of the same aisle). Each aisle is grouped and labeled by type of product and further grouped by manufacturer so the shopper can easily find what they are looking for. So think of your home as a supermarket and set it up so you can "shop at home first" before shopping at the store. More about this in chapter 10 on managing your space and inventory.

This will also help you avoid overbuying. People overbuy when they really don't know how much they have of something, or even if they have any at all. This often happens while in a store. They'll see something and can't remember if they have it or need it, and decide to "play it safe" and grab it. If it's on sale, it makes the urge to buy even greater. There is also the inner voice saying, "It won't go to waste. We can always use it." Of course, if you already have a lot of something, it means you *aren't* using it as quickly as you think you are, and you're wasting money by buying more. And now it's taking up even more space in your home.

Case in point? Once during a home office project, we gathered enough sticky notes to fill a gallon-sized plastic storage bag. When our client saw it, she raised an eyebrow and proceeded to show us a shopping bag from her trip to the office supply store *the day before*. What did it contain? Sticky notes! She had no idea she already had so many. She spent time, money, and energy buying something she already owned. Now she had to either spend more time and energy returning them (not to mention gas money) or give up space to store them even though she didn't need them.

There are two additional benefits to sorting through your belongings. At almost every organizing session, we hear the words "I was looking for that!" This is sometimes met with frustration, especially when they missed a deadline or just replaced the item thinking it was lost. But sometimes there is great relief, too! The good news is when you combine the principles of "Grouping Like with Like" with "Everything Deserves a Home," "Creating Associations," and "Finish the Task," you may never lose anything ever again!

What things have you been missing that you are excited to find?

The other added benefit is "rediscovering" some of your belongings. Along with finding things you thought were lost, you will also come across stuff you had simply forgotten you had. This can be very exciting, and a great example of how a simple mind shift can have a positive effect on the way we approach the organizing process. Think about it. Instead of focusing on what you might be *giving up*, how much different does it feel when you think of all the things you might *rediscover*?

After working with one of our clients on her clothes, she came away feeling like she had just been handed a "brand new" wardrobe. Many of the items still had tags on them! Luckily for her, this came at just the right time in the season when she could start debuting some new outfits. Even better, she didn't need to buy anything new for some events she had coming up. This is significant because she would have spent unnecessary money had she not taken steps to sort through her things and group "like with like" to see how much of everything she had.

Why this principle is important

Sorting through your belongings and grouping "like with like":

- Helps you make better, more-informed decisions because you are basing them on actual knowledge of what you have.

- Makes the purging process so much less overwhelming and more manageable.
- Prevents overbuying.
- Allows you to manage your inventory more effectively.
- Is the principle that helps make some of the others possible.

What mastering this principle will save you

Time: By sorting and grouping like items together, you will be able to quickly see how much you have in each category without spending a lot of time. You will never lose time running around the house to figure out if you need to buy more of something.

Money: You will gain a much better sense of what you have and how much you have, as well as what you need. Therefore, you will save money by not overbuying or replacing something you already own.

Energy: During the organizing process, you will save an enormous amount of physical and mental energy by handling one category at a time. Stress and anxiety deplete us of valuable energy and willpower, so making the process more manageable will help you save it for other tasks and decisions. In general, having like items together means less running around looking for things because they won't be scattered throughout the home.

Space: When you don't overbuy, you save space by not having to house unnecessary multiples. When like items are stored together, you are not using space in multiple areas to house the same category.

CHAPTER 7

Decide What Stays and What Goes

Remember when we "accidently misspoke" before and suggested that sorting through your belongings causes the most
stress? Well, we have found that it is actually this principle that
does that. It's one thing to sort through everything. It's quite
another to consciously commit to letting stuff go. After all, it's
your *stuff*. We have been given a variety of reasons and excuses
as to why people are hesitant:

- "I paid a lot of money for it."
- "I paid almost nothing for it. I got it on sale. It was a
  fantastic deal."
- "It's still good" or "There's nothing wrong with it."
- "I'm eating healthy and plan to be that size again soon."
- "My [grandmother/mother/aunt/best friend/daughter/
  son/neighbor/puppy] gave it to me."

One of the first questions potential clients ask us is "Will you make me throw everything out?" In fact, we get this question so often that we added it to the frequently asked questions (FAQ) section of our website. It's an excellent question. Here is our excellent answer:

> *No, this is a myth! It is not our goal to make you part with all of your prized possessions. Here's a simple example of how it works. You tell us you don't have enough space in your kitchen and are surrounded by clutter. If we see that you are a family of two with fifty coffee mugs, we will have a conversation about that. Then we will help you through the process of paring down. We want your space to house the things you really love and need. But don't worry, we will make sure you still have enough mugs for the ones you love. Nobody will go without coffee!*

It's interesting to note that when we talk about this part of the process, people immediately default to what they need to *give up* rather than what they may *gain*. This causes all sorts of stress. When they do focus on what they are keeping, the decision is made from a guarded and protective place, much like a child who thinks their toy is going to be taken away if they misbehave. There is a deep feeling of vulnerability. We acknowledge that vulnerability with compassion and want to support you in moving through it so it isn't the reason you are struggling with letting certain things go.

This principle pertains to what you are keeping and letting go of in general *and* regarding the space you are trying to organize. There are some things that will simply be discarded, donated, recycled, or given to friends/family. *No matter what, they are leaving your home.* Other things will be kept, *but don't belong in the space you're organizing.* Only keep things that are in line with your vision for the space. In other words, there shouldn't be socks, extra toilet paper, or power tools in the living room. These things need to be moved to other areas in your home.

This is where having a defined vision for the space (and your things already sorted) comes in handy. When it is time for the actual decision making, you are evaluating from a place of:

- Absolute knowledge of what you have and how much.
- What your vision for the room is (i.e., what the space needs to "be").

Your decisions, therefore, won't be random. They will be mindful, intentional, and with a positive and empowering goal at the center.

Let's return to our coffee mug example. If your vision for the space is to have a well-organized kitchen that makes cooking meals easy and fun, and you don't want a lot of clutter on the counters, then you may be more willing to address your extensive collection of mugs. After all, in the example, you are only two people. Even if you have a lot of friends and family over, how often are you serving coffee for fifty? You have to weigh the benefits of being able to serve so many guests against the benefit of having extra space for your more often-used items 99 percent of the time. Make sense?

Now, we realize that even when it does make sense, letting go can be hard. Like, really, really hard. We were asked to sit on a panel last year at a fundraiser for a resilience program for young girls. The question we were asked was:

> ## "Many people struggle with clutter. How can we live more fulfilled lives by embracing the power of letting go?"

This is how we answered. Note that we didn't just address physical clutter, but emotional and mental clutter as well. Often they are intertwined, and usually this is what makes it hard to let things go, even when rationally you know it would be the best choice:

So despite the rumors, professional organizers don't want you to throw everything out.

However, many people hold on to things they no longer need—mentally, physically, or emotionally. In some cases, these things are actually holding them back or preventing them from moving forward.

People can live more fulfilled lives when they are surrounded by things that make them feel good, serve a clear purpose, and help them be seen by the rest of the world as happy, confident, and hopeful.

It's important to realize that it's not just about the things themselves but what they represent that makes it so challenging, and sometimes even painful to let go: Maybe it's a time in your life when you were happier and more successful or looked better and felt more confident. Letting go may seem like you'll never feel that way again.

Let's talk about your closet ... maybe it's filled with clothes that you can't part with because "They were expensive and there's nothing wrong with them." or "It's a designer brand and you got it on sale!" ("Yay me!")

But day after day, you pick other clothes to wear. Letting go feels like failure—acknowledging a bad purchase. You convince yourself that by holding on to them, somehow you didn't waste all that money.

In reality, it's the opposite: anything you are holding on to but not using (and not selling) has no value, no matter what you paid or think you saved.

Here's another situation: you feel guilty because you inherited jewelry from your grandmother who passed away. You loved her so much, but honestly, you think her jewelry is ugly. It's not your taste and you'll never wear it. But still, you feel like you can't let it go because somehow you'd be disrespecting her, or making your parents mad.

However, it doesn't honor your grandmother to let it sit there in the back of your drawer. There are ways to love and honor her memory without holding on to physical stuff that gives you emotional baggage and not joy.

There is power in giving yourself permission to let go of the things that no longer serve you.

There is power in knowing what you have and where to find it when you need it.

There is power in being on time because you haven't lost any time looking for things.

There is power in being mindful and accepting yourself fully in this moment and letting go of conditions that you place on your happiness. "If only I had more money." "If only I could be that size again, then I'd be happy." How often do we all do that, instead of appreciating and celebrating what's going well right now? And our "stuff" sometimes feeds into this.

I'll give you an example: Say back in the day, you were a size four and now you're a size ten. You've kept your size fours as "goal clothes." You start going to the gym, eating right, and you engage in all this self-care. You start to lose weight and you look and feel great! You should feel fierce and empowered. But you don't, because you're not yet a size four. If those size four clothes make you feel like somehow you're failing instead of rocking your fitness goals, then they're not serving you. They're not motivating you. They're causing you to miss "the win." Let them go and keep moving forward. And if you get back to size four, think of all the fun you'll have shopping!

There is power in not relying on material things to make you feel happy and confident. In fact, research shows that *people who do rely on material things have higher rates of depression than those who invest in and savor experiences with friends and family.*[20, 21]

We have a client who suffers from depression who constantly buys things she wants (but has no room for) because at the time it gives her a lift. However, these things become clutter, because she has no place to store or display them. So then she feels anxious and bad about herself, which triggers another bout of depression.

There is power *in letting go of "mental clutter"—limiting beliefs and that negative mind chatter that constantly whispers to us that we're not good enough.*

To live a more fulfilled life and to show up in the world the way you want to, ask yourself: Are your things and your thoughts moving you forward or holding you back?

Give yourself permission to let go of the things that no longer serve you. It's incredibly liberating to let go of physical, mental, and emotional clutter. If you do, it can lead to increased hopefulness, happiness, and overall wellbeing.

As you can see, we understand that it's often not about the physical items at all, but what they represent. Reading this chapter won't automatically make it easier. However, we hope that it will get you thinking more intentionally about the reasons why you may be holding on to certain things. Small shifts in mindset can lead to big shifts in behavior, which then lead to new and better habits! When you are struggling with a decision, remind yourself of your goals and your vision for the space. Even Annmarie, who also helps people navigate through life transitions as a life coach, had to do this a few months ago. She shared the following on social media:

Yesterday was emotional. We let go of my father's furniture and cleared his bedroom in our home, where he lived with us for four years after he could no longer live on his own.

Yesterday, I was on the other side of the experience. I wasn't the organizer. I was the client, working through all the feelings and emotions that accompany saying goodbye to things that are fiercely personal and meaningful.

*When my Dad could no longer live on his own, we worked hard to create a living space that felt like his. We didn't want him to feel like a guest in our home, but rather that this was **his** home. I think we succeeded, which makes it harder to give his things away—even though I'm happy about where they are going—to the wonderful aide who cared for him so beautifully and a dear family friend just starting out.*

Yesterday was hard. A lot of emotions came flooding back, and I allowed myself to have them. I sat with them for a while. But to not get "stuck" in them, I also keep focused on what letting go means going forward—a walk-in closet and office, where I will practice self-care and be able to create content that helps others move forward, too. Daddy would approve.

All emotions serve a purpose. Yesterday mine reminded me how very blessed I am, and how moving forward does not mean I can't honor the past with gratitude and love.

Having a clear vision of what she wanted the space to be helped Annmarie focus on what she was building rather than what she was letting go of. In doing so, she increased her positive emotions, which allowed her to see a bigger picture. It wasn't just about having a fabulous new office space and walk-in closet; it was about what she could accomplish and create in it, and how that would translate to helping others. She knew this was something that would make her dad very happy, and that helped her let go of the things that were hard. It was bittersweet, but the sweet prevailed.

You've decided to let go . . . what's next?

When you have decided that something no longer fits your vision for the space, decide whether it will be thrown out, donated, recycled, or set aside to sell. Discard an item if it is broken, missing pieces, stained, ripped, or otherwise unsellable or unusable.

If you are donating, decide if it will be given to someone you know or a general donation center. Whichever you choose, however, *the real triumph is physically getting it out of your house once the decision has been made.* Don't give yourself any time to second guess yourself or take things back out of the bags! Tie that bag right up and put it in a holding spot for pickup or drop-off.

We completely understand why people would rather give their personal things to family and friends who will continue to use and love them. That's great! But if you aren't going to see them for a while, or they won't come pick it up, then it's still stuck in your house. Make sure the person who is receiving your generosity truly wants what you are offering and is committed to getting it from you within a reasonable timeframe. Call or text them to get confirmation. Tell them you can hold it until a specific date after which it will be donated. Otherwise, you won't be able to move forward because these things will still be taking up precious space in *your* home.

It may be disappointing if your family and friends don't wind up taking your things, but remember that you *yourself* have made the decision to let them go. Don't make your success contingent upon the actions of others. Remember that the "T" in SMART goal setting refers to the goal being timely. You've indicated which date you are willing to hold the item(s) until. So set an implementation intention: "If [Name of your loved one] doesn't pick up [the item(s)] by [date], I will add it to the general donation being picked up on [date]." Then follow through and do it. Or put the bags in your car and take them to a local donation center asap.

If you don't drive or can't get to a donation center, call for a donation pickup. Many places are looking for the very things you are parting with! Take comfort in the fact that through a general donation, you will be helping others in need.

Pro tip: If you know you are going to tackle a large organizing project, call to schedule a donation pickup before you start. Having the pickup arranged in advance will be the impetus to both start the project *and* stay on track. It will help keep you focused and motivated, and will get the bags out the door so you can better organize the stuff you are keeping.

If you prefer to sell the things you are no longer using, you have several options. From Facebook "buy and sell" groups to apps such as Poshmark and Mercari, it's never been easier to let others know what you have to offer. Of course, there is always good old eBay, consignment, and the traditional yard sale, too.

If you decide to go one of these routes, be sure that you are committed to seeing it through to the end. Sometimes our clients set things aside to sell, but what they are really doing is avoiding the decision to let go. They are so overwhelmed already that it is unrealistic to think they can handle the process of following through with a yard sale or the other options mentioned above.

Then what happens is the stuff remains there in the home, only now it's in a pile labeled "to sell." If you truly intend to sell your things, then we are all for the "to sell" pile. But just like the suggestions we gave regarding donations, give yourself a timeframe for selling the items. For example, if you are having a yard sale, schedule an actual date on the calendar and start advertising it. If you are selling online, decide how long you will wait for a sale. Set the implementation intention that if it doesn't sell within that time or by a certain date, you will donate it. Then, no matter what, get it the heck out.

What to do with the things you are keeping

When it comes to what you are keeping, consider your vision for the space: does this item align with and support what you want the space to be? Is keeping it worth the space it will be taking up in your home?

Think of the different storage areas of your home in terms of real estate. Which ones would be considered "Prime Real Estate?" These are the areas you should be storing your important, frequently used items. Often, we see Prime Real Estate being wasted on things that don't merit a prime location. Be discerning. The goal in every room or space is the same: to make it as easy as humanly possible to get what you need when you need it. The easier it is, the more time you save and the more likely you will be to keep the system in place. Evaluate your Prime Real Estate—are you using it wisely? Ask yourself, "Is it Prime Real Estate worthy?"

Years ago, when we were just starting out, we learned a valuable lesson during a kitchen project we worked on. Our client had limited storage space, and what little she had was not being used efficiently. There was a drawer that was filled with all sorts of different teas. The tea bags were all loose and mixed together. An unopened box was taking up space in a second drawer. We took all the tea, sorted it by flavor, discarded what had expired, and set it up all nicey-nice in one drawer. It looked so good! Our client thought so, too . . . and then proceeded to tell us that nobody in the household ever drinks tea! Say *what*?

Turns out they had amassed a lot of tea over the years; many boxes were gifts from other people. It never occurred to them that they should get rid of it. Why would they? It's good tea! But the reality is they don't drink tea (!), *so it didn't need to take up Prime Real Estate in their limited kitchen drawers*. It could be relocated to a different spot to be accessed only when needed.

When space is tight, don't fill it with things you aren't using; allocate it for things you truly *do* need to access. Tea, anyone?

We had made the rookie mistake of assuming they were big tea drinkers because of how much tea they had. This experience taught us never to assume, to always ask our clients what's important to them and what they are using at this point in time. It taught our client to value their Prime Real Estate and consider what is worthy of it.

Another thing to consider when deciding what to keep is acknowledging why you have certain things, particularly things that were given to you by others. Some readers aren't going to like what we are about to say next, but it's the truth:

- The fact that you inherited it from Grandma is not enough of a reason *on its own* to keep it.
- The fact that your mother brings over bags of stuff she "thinks you could use" is not enough of a reason *on its own* for you to accept them.

- The fact that it was a gift from your best friend is not enough of a reason *on its own* to keep it.

Now, before you think we completely lack compassion and sentimentality, you should know that we are actually pretty sensitive people. (Annmarie cries at commercials and is certifiably addicted to Hallmark movies. Marie—a third-degree black belt in karate, mind you—teared up throughout the college application process. Twice.)

Let us emphasize one point: We are **not** saying that you shouldn't keep these items or gifts. We **are** saying that, in and of itself, the fact that it came from a loved one is not enough of a reason on its own to keep something. It requires a conversation. It merits a "thinking through."

One of our favorite social media posts is the one we lovingly call "No, thank you.":

Repeat after us: "No, thank you."
Just because someone offers you something for free doesn't mean you are obligated to accept it, even if it's from a loved one. It's ok to say, "No, thank you. I don't need that."
Or "I have no room for that."
Or "It's beautiful, but it doesn't match my décor."
Or "It's not my style."
Always be gracious and say how much you appreciate them thinking of you. But then say it like you mean it,

"No, thank you." Because when you accept things you really don't need or want, invariably they become clutter—*your* clutter, not their clutter. Because it's out of *their* home. And now it's in yours. No, thank you.

Of course, right now we are talking about things you already own and whether you should keep it or let it go. However, if more people applied the "No, thank you" concept, they would have fewer things to evaluate. Just sayin' . . .

Also, if you have a parent who is constantly bringing things over for you to keep, whether it be family heirlooms or just "stuff," it could be *their* difficulty and resistance in letting go of things. They no longer want it in their home, so they give it to you. As a result, they feel less guilty. This is not always the case, of course, but if it is, it's important not to let their issues become yours. Recognize it for what it is with compassion, and then hold your ground. It's important for you to set your own boundaries.

Shout out to all the fellow parents out there: We would be remiss if we didn't acknowledge the fact that our kids receive an abundance of gifts from generous grandparents, aunts, uncles, and friends that extends beyond our control. These are *gifts*, so we aren't going to say "No, thank you" to the gift giver. We might return one or two, but ultimately kids today have a lot of stuff, and this is new stuff that you may not have accounted for when setting up your space. So how do you handle this excess of toys when it's not a "decide what stays and what goes" issue? We have a solution that provides several benefits.

Between holidays and birthdays, this sheer excess has led to some serious overstimulation. Many kids can't fully appreciate what they have when it's in front of them all at once. This is especially true when it's disorganized. That's why we are big fans of rotating toys. Try this: Designate a space to store some of their toys and games out of sight for a while. It can be an underutilized closet, a shelf in a back room—anywhere your kids won't see or have access to them. Leave the rest out in the area where they play. Every few months or so (you decide the timeframe), rotate out some of the toys they've been playing with and replace them with some of the ones from storage. You will be amazed at how fresh and exciting these "new" toys seem and what interest they spark. In this rare case, the concept of "out of sight, out of mind" is actually a good thing!

Kids can only focus on so much at once. They will grab what is easily accessible and forget about the rest. So you don't always know if the reason they aren't playing with something is because they aren't interested or because they just don't see it. By rotating toys, kids will have fewer items to choose from at a time and it will be easier to store and access them. You will get a much clearer picture of the types of things your kids like, and how much of it they already have. You won't be guessing, but rather coming from a place of knowledge. This is important, because you will then be able to use this information to guide your family and friends when gift-giving occasions are approaching. Some of the control is now put back in your hands. You don't want your Prime Real Estate being filled with things your kids won't ever play with, right? It's ok to tell Aunt Sarah that your child hates crafts but loves toy trucks. Often, gift givers appreciate guidance, so you will be helping them, too.

Another benefit of rotating toys is that your kids will have a greater opportunity to appreciate them. The more they play with toys they receive as gifts, the more they can connect with the gift giver. How nice would it be if your child were to think of Uncle Tommy every time he plays with the train set he got for his birthday? *This is a beautiful example of an upward spiral, when one positive behavior leads to another.*

In our experience as mothers for twenty-one years and professional organizers for close to thirteen, we have found that children become less stimulated due to the simple fact that they don't have toys at every turn in their play areas. Their eyes are not wandering all over the place to see what they can play with next. This may lead to decreased hyperactivity, and more calm, focused play. We can't always control how much kids receive as gifts from others, but we *can* manage our space in order to manage how stimulating the room is. We cover managing your space in chapter 10, but we introduced the rotating of toys in this chapter because we are asking you to make tough choices about what you are keeping in your home. We wish to support you through situations where the stuff you have is not completely within your control. After all, we parents have to stick together!

Why this principle is important

Deciding what stays and what goes:

- Allows you to use your Prime Real Estate for the things you use most often and align with your vision for the space.
- Removes things from your home that are unusable (broken/stained/missing pieces) or no longer serve you (not in line with your vision/not your taste/don't make you feel good).

What mastering this principle will save you

Time: While the decision-making process itself takes time, in the long run it will save you time. Remember that the less you have, the less you have to manage. When your space only holds what you are using, you will be able to find it quicker. It won't be lost among things that you are not using. It will also be easier to put away. This means you will not wind up spending days periodically getting back on track and having to do a whole reorganization.

Money: This principle will save you money when combined with some of the other principles. In keeping only what you need, love, and what serves you, you will be better able to manage your space and your inventory. This means less overbuying and less loss due to things becoming expired. You are setting the stage for establishing effective organization systems. In addition, instead of items sitting unused in your space—which means they have no value—you can try to sell them and recoup some of what you originally spent.

Energy: When you hold on to things for the wrong reasons, the negative energy can take a toll. As we mentioned, negative emotions narrow and focus and lead to downward spirals. Being honest with yourself and keeping things for the right reasons will feel empowering, increase positive emotions, and lead to a "broaden and build" mindset.[22] You will feel energized and optimistic, and you will not become depleted. You will have more positive energy for important decisions and willpower to stay on course.

Space: This principle really saves you space because you are letting go of things you aren't using but were taking up valuable space. Less wasted space means more opportunity to use the space you do have for what you really need and will open up a lot of organizing opportunities that weren't there before.

CHAPTER 8

Everything Deserves a Home

Sometimes all you need is a good mantra. Here's ours: *Everything deserves a home.*

This is the concept that started it all for us, the idea we kept going back to as busy moms trying to stay afloat in a sea of toys and paperwork. Before having kids, we both had successful careers in other fields. We both managed people, our time, daunting to-do lists, and seemingly impossible deadlines. So why was it that there were toys in the kitchen and the daily mail was trying to drown us?

It's amazing how much clutter can annoy you when you are home all day to see it.

So we did what any great friends do—we called each other up and complained. A lot. Then we brainstormed. A lot. It always came back to the idea of giving everything we owned its own home.

No matter what we do or where we go, at some point we come back *home*. We go grocery shopping, or to work, or to our children's games and then we come *home*. We don't sleep on the corner, ring a stranger's bell, or just randomly stop driving the car. We come where? Say it with us, friends! *Home*. And most days, the majority of us don't get lost.

So, imagine how much easier everyday life would be if you just applied this principle to your *stuff*. When everything has a home, and gets returned to that home, there's no guesswork. There's no time wasted looking for things. You can find what you need when you need it.

Theoretically, *there would be no clutter*. #canyouimagine?

Running around the house in a last-minute panic looking for something you need to take with you? *Not pretty*. Losing important documents because there are piles of paper everywhere? *Not cool*. Spending time and money to replace "lost" items or expired food? *Not cheap*. Who has all this extra time and money? Not us, for sure. And we certainly don't have the extra energy!

And guess what? If you are a parent, you can and *should* apply this principle to your children's things, even if they're too young to know what a principle is. If they don't want to lose their favorite toy, then they should have a specific home for it and return it when they are done using it. If it gets lost, the onus should be on them. Having specific homes for their things will teach them from a young age how to respect and keep track of them. It will assist them with time management. It will serve them well in school and in life. Also, you will avoid meltdowns, and we don't just mean *theirs*.

Marie shares a real-life example:

Long before my teenagers started college, they were little pre-schoolers trained by their teachers to put everything away when "mat time" was over. The classroom had an open floor plan, but it was sectioned off for different activities, like drawing/painting, building blocks, playing house, puzzles and games, story time/show & tell, etc. These kids were like well-oiled machines in the classroom; they knew exactly where to find things and where to return them. More than that, they knew it was expected that they should put things back properly when they were done using them. My two were more than happy to be the teacher's pet and help during clean up time. They felt very proud and competent. It was really quite adorable.

That is, until they got dismissed. When I would get them home, the teachers' well-oiled machines would morph into bats out of hell—dumping their school bags, artwork, and toys all over the house. They were hyper. I was yelling! Sh*t was getting real.

One constant struggle involved those darn little toys my kids would get from vending machines at the bowling alley or places like Chuck E. Cheese. They would constantly misplace them. You might be thinking, "So what? They're cheap. Just replace them." That's not the point. To my kids, they had value . . . intrinsic value! When they were missing, they thought the world was literally ending. This would invariably happen right before we needed to leave for one of their activities, like swim class. The stress to find their precious toys would affect all of us. I would get aggravated because we would now be late for their pricey one-on-one swim lessons. My kids would get upset and lose their enthusiasm for something they usually enjoyed. Fingers would get pointed and voices would get raised—all because of a little toy that was never properly put away.

I knew I needed to nip this in the bud before things got totally out of hand. Clearly, they were capable since they did exactly what they were supposed to do at school. I decided to take a page out of their teachers' lesson plan and create zones to house (and separate) their stuff.

We had two junk drawers in our coffee table that didn't have a clear purpose. I cleaned them out and assigned one to each child. It was a personal space to house their special little toys and trinkets that didn't have a home like the "real" toys in the playroom. They were each responsible and accountable for what was in their specific drawer. The kids loved it and so did I! My table was no longer cluttered, and more importantly, there were no more tears, stress, or blame. Even in a rush, they could easily find a last-minute toy to bring with them. When they couldn't find something, well, that was on them.

The result: The kids learned what my expectations were and had a clear "home" for those special things they didn't want anyone else to touch. They respected their personalized spaces and quickly learned that "everything deserves a home."

Our simple challenge for testing this principle: Take an item you lose frequently, such as your keys or sunglasses, and establish a definitive home for it. For the next two weeks, consciously focus your attention and energy on returning that item to its home when you are done using it. Be consistent and diligent. Ask family members to help you stay on point. As time goes on, this new learned behavior will become second nature. Watch how you no longer lose the item at all!

Why this principle is important

Establishing a home for something allows you to:

- Find it when you need it, immediately and without stress.
- Easily put it away when you are done using it (so you can find it again next time!).

What mastering this principle will save you

Time: You will not lose time looking for things. You know where it should be and you either have it or you don't. There's no need to run all over the house in a panic. You will also save time by not going to the store or shopping online to replace something you already own simply because you can't find it.

Money: Why buy it twice? You will not waste money replacing something you already have, or on the extra gas you will need driving to and from the stores.

Energy: It is exhausting trying to find things when you don't know exactly where they are, especially when you are in a rush. Having to replace something you need costs more than time and money. It depletes us of valuable energy. It is also very frustrating and disheartening. Negative emotions are "heavier" and more draining than positive emotions, and ultimately affect our mood and feelings of being in control.

Space: We all struggle finding room for the stuff we actually need and use. Having unnecessary duplicates requires more space to house them. Not having these duplicates means that space can be used for important things you do own.

CHAPTER 9

Create Associations Between Your Things and Where They Live

If you wanted to cook a nice meal, how enjoyable would it be if your pots were in one room, your spatula in another, your condiments were upstairs, etc.? If you had to run and gather things from many different places every time you wanted to cook, would you even bother? No, because it would be a time-and-energy-depleting chore, and it would be annoying. This is why (most) people keep everything related to everyday cooking in the kitchen.

This seems like a silly example, right? *Of course* these things go in the kitchen. Everyone knows that! Why would we ever keep them anyplace else?

Yet for so many categories, this is exactly what we do. We don't keep "like items" together, we don't store them in a convenient place to where we are using them, and not everyone in the house knows where these categories can be found. The result of this is a lot of running around, unnecessary buying and frustration, not to mention wasted time, money, and energy.

The reason why we keep cooking-related items in the kitchen is because we were taught to do so: by our parent or guardian, by society, by the nice chef on TV. It's not something we even need to think about; it has been ingrained in our brains for as long as we can remember.

In other words, *we have a very clear and specific association between items used for cooking and the kitchen.*

This particular example is so clear that it's reasonable to assume this same association exists in other people's kitchens as well. If we were visiting a friend and needed a spatula, we might not know exactly where in the kitchen to find it, but we would certainly assume it's somewhere in the kitchen. We wouldn't start the search in the bathroom, garage, or family room. (At least we hope not!)

In our chapter discussing how to "Sort Through Your Belongings and Group 'Like with Like'," we talk about the benefits of keeping like items together. When you engage in the sorting process, you become aware of all the different categories you have.

"Everything Deserves a Home" is a more conceptual principle—understanding that you want to give your things a designated place to return to and all the reasons why.

"Creating Associations" is the principle that works hand in hand with these others and takes your chances for success to the next level.

Here's how it works: For each category you have, designate *one* specific "home" for it and then mindfully create the association between the two.

For example, all your tools should be in one place. All your utility items should be in another (batteries, lightbulbs etc.). Anyone who picks up the mail should place it in your family's designated mail spot until it can be addressed (preferably daily). There shouldn't be five places where you have piles of paper, or piles of anything for that matter. Your house and car keys? *One* spot.

Here's another important point: Everyone in your household should make the *same* association, so that everyone knows exactly where to look when they need something. There's no looking in five different places where it *might* be, because "such and such" category is located *here*.

- "I need a lightbulb." *Lightbulbs are in the hall closet.*
- "I need paper towels." *Extra paper towels are on the shelving unit in the basement.*
- "I need a C battery." *Batteries are in the junk drawer.*

If you associate *one* place in your home for a specific category, you will save a *lot* of time looking for things you need. This is particularly helpful when you are in a rush. Have you heard of the phrase "running around like a chicken without a head?" Annmarie had one such chicken:

My daughter Julianna is a beautiful and accomplished young college student now. But just a few years ago, before she fully grasped how magnificent a blessing it was to have a mother who is a professional organizer, she was a typical teenager who didn't think I knew anything. That is, until she couldn't find something. Then she expected me to know everything. Given what I did for a living, it was very hard to watch her room reach the catastrophic level of mess that it did. It took every ounce of patience and fortitude to take other parents' advice and just "shut the door." Inevitably there were times that I really didn't know where her things were because she had no particular home for them, except occasionally the floor. So I couldn't help her when she lost something.

There was more than one occasion where she was late for school or some other event because she couldn't find what she needed. She would literally run around the house in a panic, desperately searching in vain for the missing item. Even when she did eventually find it, it had such a negative effect on her mood, personality, and ability to communicate. It made her feel bad about herself and manifested itself in words and actions that made her look defensive. Throw hormones into that mix and let me tell you, we had ourselves a situation.

I'm happy to report that over time, Julianna began to realize that she had more control over her life than she thought. While she couldn't control everything, she could take ownership of her things and how she managed them. Something clicked, and positive changes started to happen. She began to *embrace many of the organizing concepts I would teach her. She became more mindful about how she grouped things and where she put each category in her room. It's important to note that she didn't group the same way I would have, and that's okay! The categories and where she decided to put them made perfect sense to her.*

In terms of our family organization, she became familiar with the associations we had created for our things. If she needed a battery, she would go to the junk drawer in the kitchen. If we had the size she needed, she could just take it and continue on without relying on anyone else. If she needed an extra binder, she knew that we kept a bin of extra school supplies in the family room closet. If there wasn't a binder in there, she knew she would need to go to the store and buy one.

Now I'm sad because my little chickie is away at school, but I'm happy because she took all these principles and applied them to her dorm room. It helps her be responsible and show up confidently at school and in life. As a parent, it's very exciting to watch your child become empowered like that.

When you associate a category with a location, it's like having your own internal GPS system. When you or your family needs to find something, your GPS eliminates the rest of the house or space and guides you to its exact location. Hence, there's less running around and less energy expended. For example, if you associate batteries with the kitchen junk drawer, you won't need to search your entire house for them. Your internal GPS will lead you right to that kitchen drawer. You will know instantly when you open it whether you have batteries or not. No wasted time searching, and no wasted money replacing them if you already have them. Narrowing your search saves time, money, and energy while reducing stress!

Which brings us back to the "I was looking for that!" concept on page 78 of the "Sort Through Your Belongings and Group 'Like with Like'" chapter. We weren't kidding. Nine out of ten times, someone will say a variation of this line during an organizing session. And as we mentioned, this often happens during the sorting process. That's why we introduced it in that chapter. But here's the kicker:

"Creating Associations" is the key to never having to utter the words "I was looking for that!" again.

Most likely, the reason our clients couldn't find their "lost" items was simply because they hadn't known where to search. They hadn't made the connection between which category the item belonged in and where that category "lived" in their home. Think how much easier life would be if we made these connections regularly. How much time could you save if you didn't lose precious time looking for things you know you have . . . somewhere? More importantly, what would you do with that extra time?

Imagine the possibilities.

It has become quite customary to complain about not having enough hours in the day, or days in the week, to get everything done. But there is actually a lot of time that is lost—ironically—looking for things that are "lost," or more accurately, misplaced.

Just like Annmarie's daughter realized, while we can't control everything, we can control some things.

- We can't control our boss scheduling an unexpected meeting, *but we can control knowing where important paperwork is for that meeting.*

- We can't control a storm knocking out power to our home, *but we can control knowing exactly where to find the candles, matches, flashlights, and batteries.*

- We can't control a medical emergency, *but we can control where we keep the first aid supplies or important insurance information for the ER.*

Reflection: Think of a recent situation where you felt either out-of-control or like you didn't have your act together. What happened and how did you feel during that time? How could "creating associations" have led to a more positive outcome?

This principle can also be used to determine in which category an item should go in the first place. When grouping "like with like," we recommend categorizing your items based on *how you use them*, not just what they are.

Some examples:

- If you only use onion soup mix to make onion dip, then it's not necessary to group it with cans or containers of the soup you actually eat. Group it with other dips and dip mixes.

- If you only use Q-tips to clean the grooves in your furniture, keep them with cleaning supplies instead of your health & beauty products.

- If you only use baby wipes to remove deodorant stains from your clothing (it works!), then keep them in your clothes closets or dresser drawers.

The categories have to make sense to you and your family. If you associate correctly, you will be more likely to find what you need when you need it, which in the end is the whole point! Know that where one family keeps a certain category may be different than where another family keeps the same category. For example, Annmarie's batteries are in her kitchen junk drawer, while Marie's are in her basement storage area. Annmarie's holiday decorations are in her attic;

Marie's are in her garage. Since each family has created the associations for their household, the principle works for both families!

Why this principle is important

Creating associations:

- Allows you to know at once where to look for something you need, even if you were not the one to purchase the item in the first place.
- Fosters independence in children (and spouses!) who won't have to rely on you to find what they need.
- Makes it very easy to put new purchases away.
- Reduces the chances of misplacing things because you have a very clear association between the item and where in your home it can be found.

What mastering this principle will save you

Time: Having a clear association about where your different categories live is like having your own GPS system. It means you can eliminate the entire rest of the house or space and go straight to one location to find what you are looking for. The less time you spend looking for things, the more time you will have to get other tasks done or even just have fun!

Money: Similar to the other principles, anytime you don't have to spend money replacing things you already own but can't find, it's a good thing! You save money on the item itself, plus not wasting gas means filling up your tank less frequently.

Energy: This is probably the most impactful thing you save with this principle. Remember the "running around like a chicken without a head" reference? Eliminating that scenario saves an enormous amount of physical, mental, and emotional energy. Plus, the negative emotions that accompany feeling frantic and overwhelmed are extremely draining.[23] Mastering this principle will help you feel more confident and in control, and you will in turn feel energized and empowered. In essence, you will be gaining positive, forward-moving energy and reducing negative, draining energy!

Space: When you replace items you 1) think you have lost, or 2) can't find but still have, you are housing more than you need. The drawback is that this takes space away from other things you do need. Additionally, it's not just about the amount of space you save, but rather where you are saving it. When your categories are each in a specific location, other areas in the home aren't housing random items that should all be together somewhere else. This will make organizing these other spaces easier and more beneficial to you, because you can devote the whole space to whatever categories belong there.

CHAPTER 10
Manage Your Space (So You Can Manage Your Inventory)

Let's start this chapter with a pop quiz! Don't worry—it's only one question:

Do you manage your space based on your inventory or your inventory based on your space?

If you said the latter, you win a brand-new car! Okay not really, but you *are* correct! Your space should determine how much inventory (things/belongings/household items/clothing/stuff) you have. You may remember from chapter 3 that clutter develops for many reasons. One of those reasons is buying first and worrying about space later.

When you only have a certain amount of space to house a particular category, and you overbuy in that category, the simple fact is that it will not fit. We have worked some mighty fine miracles in helping clients maximize their space and rethink how they organize within it. However, one thing we cannot do is conjure space from thin air (although imagine if we had *that* superpower!).

Take batteries as an example. Let's assume you've followed the principles in Chapters 8 and 9. You've given them a designated home in a kitchen junk drawer and created a clear association between the two. What happens when you overbuy and the amount you now have exceeds that space? The rest of it has to go *somewhere*. Two possible options:

1. You don't do anything with the extra batteries because you don't know where they should go. Therefore, depending upon where you leave them, they become that room's clutter.
2. You put them in a second location, such as your closet. This means you have to create more than one association about where to find them.

Now let's fast forward a few months. You need four batteries but there are only two in the junk drawer. You may have forgotten about the extras you purchased all those months ago and assume you've run out. Worse, you might go to the store and buy them, wasting time, money, and energy. Not to mention, you now need space to store the replacements—which aren't needed in the first place because you have more in the closet! The irony of this is almost ridiculous.

Establishing a home for your things is essential. Deciding how much space you are willing to allocate for a particular category is equally essential.

It's very easy to lose sight of what you have and where it is when you don't intentionally and consciously 1) monitor your space, and 2) make buying decisions accordingly. If you've already sorted through your things and grouped "like with like," this step is much easier to set up and put into practice.

For example, no matter how great a sale on pasta is at the grocery store, Annmarie will not buy more than what will fit within a certain amount of space in her pantry. She will not take space away from her other pantry items to accommodate the extra. She will not put them on other shelves within the pantry because then they won't be grouped "like with like" and she will lose track of what she has. She won't put them in other places outside the pantry for the same reason.

Marie makes buying decisions at Costco based on freezer space:

I'll know I need to buy a bag of frozen mixed vegetables because it's on my list. My dilemma? I'd like to buy four 5-pound bags of it because they are on sale, and the limit is four. It's a great deal, but I will still talk myself out of it because I know there is not enough room to accommodate those four big bags in my freezer. "Grouping Like with Like" within my freezer helps me to shop accordingly and manage both inventory and space. So instead of buying four because the big warehouse chain is subliminally telling me, as the consumer, that my limit is only four, I think it through and logically only buy two. By the time those bags are used up at home, there is usually another sale.

In order to control your space, you need to make a conscious decision about how much you are willing to allocate for a particular category. Marie was not willing to take up most of her limited freezer space with multiples of one item.

Another great example was a kids' playroom we organized years ago for a family with four young children. The space was a decent size, but you couldn't even see the floor because it was filled with toys and games. The children could never focus on playing with one toy at a time since they were so overstimulated. They really had nowhere to sit and play, so they would often take their toys to other parts of the home. There was an excess of every kind of toy, including an enormous collection of Barbie dolls that filled three large bins. The youngest daughter was so attached to her Barbies that her mother was sure that she would never part with any of them. Had they had an infinite amount of space, perhaps three bins would not have been a problem. However, this one room had to accommodate toys for four children, without using the floor as storage space!

So, with the mother's permission, Marie took this little four-year-old girl aside and sat her next to one empty bin. She explained that we were hoping to create a wonderful playroom for her and her siblings and that we needed to create more space so that everything wasn't thrown all over the floor. They also talked about how other, less-fortunate children would love to have some Barbies.

Marie told the little girl to really think about which of the Barbies were her absolute favorites and to put them in the bin. Whatever could fit in the bin with the lid on, she could keep. Not only did she stay within one bin, but also just filled it three quarters of the way through! When Marie told her there was still room for a few more, she said it wasn't necessary. She had all she needed.

This story illustrates a few points:

- The importance and effectiveness of deciding in advance how much space you are willing to allocate.
- When we have to be more mindful of what we can keep, we make more well-thought-out decisions about what's really important to us and why.
- *We underestimate kids all the time.*

In the end, this family still had more than enough toys, but they also regained control of their space. And while we are on the subject of toys, don't forget the strategy of rotating toys that we discussed in Chapter 7. Rotating toys has many benefits, including managing your space effectively.

Overbuying
The problems associated with overbuying cannot be over-emphasized.

Sometimes people overbuy when things are on sale because they sincerely believe they are saving money for their family. But consider this: If you buy a shirt on super sale but never wear it because you can never find it, guess how much money you've saved? Zero.

If you catch a super sale at the market and buy twenty of [insert item name here] when you really only need two, and after a few years you still haven't consumed them and they expire so you have to throw them out, guess how much money you've saved? Zero.

Some people are naturally attracted to the thrill of the deal, but here's the real deal: It's only a deal if you use what you've bought. Otherwise, you've spent money, not saved it.

Remember the sticky note story from the "Like with Like" chapter? Our client already had a lot of sticky notes but they weren't grouped together and managed in a particular space. As a result, when she was at the store, she bought more because she couldn't remember if she had any, and didn't want to take a chance. It was easier just to "play it safe" and buy more. She rationalized this decision in two ways:

- "It's a relatively small item. They don't take up much space."
- "We can always use sticky notes. They won't go to waste."

However, neither reason is the point. The reality is that an unnecessary purchase was made because of poor inventory and space management.

Now, is this one instance of excess sticky notes the end of the world? Of course not. However, in our client's small apartment, the extra space needed to house the extra *was* relevant. With her challenging financial situation, the extra money spent *was* relevant. This was one incident, but when you have multiple and regular incidences of overbuying and unnecessary spending, it adds up. We have simplified the example for teaching purposes, but clutter and disorganization are often a compilation of many of these examples that happen regularly and simultaneously.

Even when there is a major sale, pause and take a moment to think what overbuying might *cost* you. You may realize that the cost in the long run will ultimately outweigh the short-term savings.

Of course, sometimes there are other factors at play, like when Annmarie's dad went crayon shopping at Staples years ago:

Before my dad came to live with us on Long Island, he lived in Brooklyn and was still self-sufficient and mobile. My daughter was in first grade, and it came time to do our back-to-school shopping. Staples was running this incredible sale on RoseArt® crayons. They were $0.05 a box and you could only buy five boxes at a time. Well, Daddy made it his mission to buy as many boxes as possible, going back to the store several times in the process. It became a game for him, as well as a way to pass the time and socialize. When he was done, we *had enough crayons to supply every classroom in the school! The cost of the gas he used in driving back and forth probably exceeded the savings, but wow, did he feel proud and happy that he could buy my daughter crayons. I didn't have the heart to say anything, and I certainly didn't teach him anything about managing inventory. I simply sent in extra boxes to the teachers each year, and never had to buy crayons again. Daddy passed away in 2015, but my daughter's crayon supply lasted all through elementary, middle, and high school.*

I still have one box left. XO.

Recognizing that this may not be the right story to encourage you not to overbuy, we include it to show that we understand that things aren't always as simple as they seem and to emphasize an important organizing concept: *shopping at home first.*

In all seriousness, "The Great Crayon Adventure" was an isolated incident. In general, Annmarie's dad did *not* constantly overbuy or give her things she didn't need. For that reason, she was able to go with the flow and not allow it to derail her organizing systems. In deciding to indulge her dad's sweet shopping extravaganza, she relied upon the organizing principles in this book. She grouped the crayons with extra school supplies, established a home for where she kept this category, and created an association between the two. Extra school supplies are housed in a bin in her family room closet. Everyone knows where to go if they need something. If they have it, it's there. If not, it goes on the shopping list. Either way, the family shops at home first.

In the case of the crayons, Annmarie would take her daughter's school supply list and—say it with us, friends!—*shop at home first*. In this way, she wouldn't buy things she already had, like crayons! Whatever she didn't have would go on her shopping list. Approaching it in this way allowed her to shop from a place of knowledge and confidence, and prevented impulse buys and unnecessary spending. It also conserved her space, because she was using down what she had, rather than increasing the space needed by buying too much.

When setting up a space, we would invite you to consider the following:

Is this space considered "Prime Real Estate?"

Back in the "Decide What Stays and What Goes" chapter, we introduced you to the concept of Prime Real Estate. In the world of professional organizing, these are areas that are easily accessible, and where you should be storing your important, often-used items. We gave a real example of a client who had been using two main drawers in her kitchen to store tea bags, when no one in the family even drank tea! In the meanwhile, she had a lot of clutter, because things the family *was* using had no place to be stored. When you are organizing a particular space, we invite you to think about where it is located, how easy it is to access, and whether or not you should consider it Prime Real Estate. If it is Prime Real Estate, think about the things you wish to store there—are they worthy of such a space?

In our tea example, the tea was simply unworthy of that particular space. They were serving tea "once in a blue moon." It was good tea, fine to keep in another location within or near the kitchen. But our client needed that prime location for things she needed to access daily or often.

In our section on rotating toys, we said that having an excess of them in one area is not a good use of Prime Real Estate. The toys *themselves* might be worthy, just not *all* at the same time. It makes it difficult to see, access, and appreciate everything in that one specific space. Plus, it will help avoid the spillover of toys into another space nearby. It can also cause overstimulation. By rotating toys, you have less to manage within the space, giving you more options for setting up the room to align with your vision and goals for your children. It also gives you more clarity about your children's likes and dislikes, and knowledge with which to guide family and friends regarding gifts.

Are you using your Prime Real Estate wisely?

How often are you accessing the items?

Things you don't need to access often should not be stored in prime locations. They can be placed on upper, harder-to-reach shelves or stored in lesser-used spaces, such as in your attic.

If something is used daily or several times a week, then it should be very accessible. An organized space is meant to make your life easier to manage, so having to expend a lot of energy to get something is very frustrating! These are the things that should go in your Prime Real Estate storage locations—closets, cabinets, and drawers that don't require a step stool.

Sometimes when we move into a new home, there is pressure to get unpacked and functional in a very short period of time. As a result, new homeowners often just put their things away without much thought in an effort to just get up and running. Yes, they will put kitchen stuff in the kitchen (hopefully!), but they might not think it through any further than that due to exhaustion and stress. This is why it's important to make mindful, intentional decisions. It also gives credence to the strategy of planning out a space and creating clear zones.

Without an intentional focus on how you are setting things up, your behavior becomes contingent upon the set-up, leaving you less in control.

When Annmarie and her family moved into their new home eighteen years ago, they did what we described above—moved in and unpacked. They had a lot they were dealing with, and they had to get back to work while also taking care of their infant daughter. They got everything out of the boxes, but there was a bare minimum of planning beyond toiletries being placed in the bathroom, towels being placed in the linen closet, etc.

One day, when Annmarie went to go replace the toilet paper in her main bathroom, she had an "a-ha" moment:

I bent down towards the very bottom shelf to get a roll and when I stood back up, I was eye level with a whole bunch of toiletries that I almost never accessed—they were extras and not needed on a regular basis. I thought to myself, "Why in the world am I bending down for toilet paper, which I need fairly regularly, when I could just store them at eye level? It would be so much easier, and much better for my back, too!"

After that, she completely reassessed her space and how she had filled it, and reorganized it in a way that made sense for what she needed on a regular basis. She started reevaluating her other spaces, too. We have come to call this idea "conscious organizing," and it is a real game changer.

What goals do you associate with this space?

This is really important, because the organizing you do should always support the way in which you want to live and how you wish to show up in the world.

If you work long hours and your goal is to rest and recharge each evening, make your bedroom your "sanctuary." We suggest clearing the room of anything business or task-related, including paperwork and laptops. Even when we don't use or handle these items, seeing them in the space sends the subliminal message that we are still working, "plugged in," and accessible. The point is to free your mind of work reminders. The fewer you have in your bedroom, the calmer you will feel.

If you are a parent and your goal is to foster independence in your children, then you want to make it as easy as possible for them to access their things, as well as put them away! For example, when setting up a space for their toys, place things you want them to grab independently at eye level, so they can see and reach them easily. If your goal is also to teach them that certain things require your permission, place these things you wish to control (Play-Doh, permanent markers, and puzzles with 1000 pieces!) up high where they can't be reached without your assistance.

If your goal is to eat healthier, place fruits and vegetables and other healthy foods in your refrigerator at eye level. You are more likely to grab them when they are kept right in front of you. Make it as easy as possible to see and access them![24]

Remember that "eye level is buy level." Retail stores do this all the time. They put the more expensive merchandise they want you looking at right at eye level.[25] They put other, less-important items on higher and lower shelves. This is subliminal, and absolutely intentional. They also put things right by the register to grab your attention as you are waiting in line. Impulse buying is legit!

Are you storing items with a shelf life?

Two words: expiration dates! One of the biggest advantages some readers of this book will enjoy is the money that will be saved on expired food and medication. We cannot tell you how many thousands of dollars in expired products we have found in our clients' homes and had to throw right into the garbage. It is painful each and every time and can be prevented by simply employing the principles you are learning here.

When setting up a pantry (or food cabinet if you don't have a pantry), the first step is to group like items together so that your categories are clear. Try to do this at a time when you have gone shopping and have a fairly accurate representation of how much you usually have in each category. In other words, don't make space decisions when your cupboards are bare.

Similar to a supermarket set-up, if you have duplicates of items, line them up one behind the other, in order of when they will expire (soonest date in front). When you see the one in front, there will be no guesswork as to what's behind it. You will know that the ones that follow are the same in type and flavor.

Examples:

- Containers of the same type of broth (all low-sodium chicken, all beef, etc.)
- Boxes of the same type of pasta (all penne, all farfalle, all spaghetti, etc.)
- Cans of the same type of tomatoes for sauce (all whole, all crushed, all peeled, etc.)

If you have multiples of the same category that are slightly different, placing them one behind the other won't work the same way as when the items are identical. Looking at the one in front won't tell you what's behind it because they aren't all the same. In this case, we recommend using a clear pantry bin to create a "drawer" on the shelf. Place the items in the bin (also by expiration date) and label the category. When you need to get something, pull the bin out like a drawer, take what you need, and slide the bin back in. In this way, you won't create an avalanche trying to reach something in the back. There also won't be any dead space in the back, and therefore no "abyss" for things to get lost in or forgotten about.

Examples:

- Containers of different types of spices (garlic powder, oregano, red pepper flakes, etc.)
- Cans of different flavored soups (chicken noodle, vegetable, cream of mushroom, etc.)
- Different types of condiments (ketchup, mustard, relish, etc.)

This same technique works great in other areas of your home, too. For example, use a clear, plastic bin in your refrigerator to store different flavored yogurts or juice boxes; use one in your freezer to corral bags of frozen vegetables or ice pops.

You can also apply this strategy to your medicine cabinet, grouping meds for different ailments together (allergy, pain, cold/cough, first aid etc.). Highlight expiration or "discard" dates so you can easily keep track. We've disposed of a lot of expired meds, too! Taking expired drugs may be unsafe, or at the very least less effective (which in some cases could actually be dangerous!). Keeping your categories separate and easily accessible will help you manage your medication more effectively.

Inventory and overflow

When it comes to managing your inventory, the premise is the same whether there is a shelf life or not. Within the space you are organizing, like items should be grouped together and categories should be placed strategically to maximize visibility and accessibility. You should have clear associations about where things reside in general (e.g., in which closet) as well as where they reside within that space (e.g., which shelf within that closet and on which side). You may know that all of your utility items are in your basement closet. Yet, within that closet, you might establish that light bulbs specifically reside on the second shelf to the left. In doing so, even within the smaller space, you can go right to the place where they should be and see if you have them. You won't have to disturb anything on the other shelves guessing if it's there because your association will be so strong that you will be confident in your answer.

If you do have them, great! You've found them quickly and without expending a lot of energy. If you don't have them, then you know you need to put it on your list. Of course, as you become adept at managing your space and inventory, you will be able to create a system where you will never be without what you need. As you get to a certain level of inventory, you will add it to the list before you run out.

For example, here's how Marie manages her paper goods:

My husband and I like to buy paper goods in bulk, and we have an area in our basement where we keep the "overflow."

Overflow is the extra that is leftover after we have stocked other areas in our home. I will stock my three bathrooms with toilet paper, and the rest will live in my basement closet in my "overflow area." I will continue to re-stock my bathrooms from this basement overflow area as needed, but when I run low on inventory in the basement, that's when I put it on my list. In doing it this way, I never get caught without toilet paper in the bathrooms themselves (awkward!). By the time I have to replenish again, I will have stocked up my overflow area once more. This system works just right for us because we have very clear associations and we manage our space well.

Now you are seeing how these principles, while important on their own, weave together to create beautiful and seamless organizing systems that work.

Focus on folding

When trying to manage your drawer space, consider different ways of folding your clothes to maximize space. For example, we have several clients who simply don't have the closet space to hang their jeans. Depending on the dimensions of their drawers, sometimes we fold them in half, other times we fold them "in threes" to get the most out of the space they have. The same is true for non-clothing items such as towels and sheets. Some people prefer to roll their towels rather than fold them. Some fold their sheets and then store them within a matching pillow case. Experiment with different folding to match the depth and width of your shelving. Some minor adjustments might make all the difference!

You may also wish to consider "vertical folding," which allows you to store things like t-shirts on their side, similar to files in a file cabinet. It's not for everyone, because it does require a commitment to folding that way consistently. However, for the willing, it has a lot of benefits, particularly the ability to see different patterns, designs, or logos with ease. This allows you to access what you need instantly, without rummaging. You can use this method for other categories, too. For example, Annmarie folds and stores her dish towels vertically. There is a how-to video on our website if you're interested in learning this folding technique.

We also have a video on how to fold plastic bags like you would fold an American flag to save space. (Yes, there really is a video for everything!) It's a cool trick Marie learned from her mother, who learned it from her cousin in Italy. In fact, we got a lot of positive comments and messages, many from others with Italian relatives who do the same thing. (Is this an Italian thing?) Like vertical folding, it's not for everyone, but for some it's worth the effort. Annmarie repurposes supermarket bags to use as "poopie bags" when she walks her dog, so for her it's a great space saver. She is literally able to contain fifty supermarket bags in a small bin in her pantry. It all comes back to finding what works for you and your family, and trying different tips and strategies until you do.

Convenience and accessibility

Managing your space and what goes in it should always make your life easier. If you want a short-sleeve white shirt, you should be able to go to your closet and find where all your short-sleeve shirts are hung. It's either there or it's in the laundry. It shouldn't be mixed in with your sweaters or pants or sweat-shirts. In terms of managing your closet or drawer space, you would use the Prime Real Estate areas to house the types of clothing you access most often. For some that means corporate work apparel. For others that means jeans and tees. Having the things you wear most often in accessible locations will help you make better buying decisions about what you need. It will also increase the percentage of clothing you actually wear!

Even within a drawer, set up clear zones and group your categories accordingly. If you need a certain t-shirt, there should be no guesswork about which drawer to look in. If you can't fit all your t-shirts in the drawers, you will have to make a decision: Do you take space away from another category to accommodate the t-shirts? Are they that important?

If they are, then you must reduce the space you need for other categories *or* you need to let go of another t-shirt so the amount of space you need remains the same. "When something comes in, something else must go out." Otherwise you are guaranteeing that you will have clutter, because there are things that will be homeless. Homeless things wind up in places like the floor, dresser tops, tables, the floor (yes, we know we said it twice.).

This brings us back to the very beginning of the chapter where we said that managing your space is the key to managing your inventory. It should be a driving force behind buying decisions and a mindful process that keeps you in control. The organizing should drive the behavior, and when done successfully, it will drive *positive* behavior that will enhance the quality of your life.

A final note about space

Sometimes in the organizing process, you might find yourself with (gasp!) an empty space. Perhaps you've pared down your categories and the homes you've established are spacious enough to accommodate what you have.

It's okay to leave that space empty. *Don't fill a space just to fill it.* Live with the empty space for a little while so you can figure out what items are worthy of it, especially if it's part of your Prime Real Estate. Inevitably something will come to mind that is worthy, and it will make sense as to why you put it there. Your decision will once again be made from a place of mindful, conscious organizing. The association you create will be stronger and more effective because the decision was intentional rather than random or desperate.

Why this principle is important

Managing your space and your inventory:

- Allows you to maintain control of how much you have and how much you spend.

- Prevents overbuying.
- Eliminates the clutter that comes from overbuying and not having a place to store it all.
- Prevents waste by ensuring that things don't expire before you consume them.
- Leads to "conscious organizing" and mindful decision making.

What mastering this principle will save you

Time: By managing your space, your categories will stay intact, making it very easy for you to find what you need quickly. By setting yourself up to shop at home first, you will save time by not shopping for things you already own. You will spend less time in the stores because your lists will be accurate and likely shorter since they will not contain unnecessary items.

Money: Managing your space and shopping at home first means less overbuying, even when there is a super sale, because you know how much space you are willing to allocate for something. This saves money in two ways: 1) less spending in the first place, and 2) less money wasted from things expiring.

Energy: When you have a handle on your space and how you manage it, you will spend less energy looking for and accessing what you need. Plus, it will be much easier to put things away. You will not make unnecessary shopping trips, and there will be fewer decisions to make. As a result, this means less mental energy will be expended.

Space: Shopping at home first means you are using down what you already have "in stock." Therefore, you save space by not having to accommodate items you purchase unnecessarily. Not filling a space "just to fill it" means you will be saving it for what's truly important and what serves you and your family best. Rotating toys helps avoid spillover into other rooms because the play area isn't overcrowded; you are controlling how much is in there at any one time.

CHAPTER 11
Finish the Task!

Sometimes, it's not that people don't know what to do. It's not even that they don't *do* what they're supposed to do. They do, but *only to a certain point*. They don't take that extra step to fully complete the task. They get to that certain point and then they just . . . stop.

Finishing the task means seeing it through to the very end. There's a reason why a long or seemingly never-ending to-do list causes people to feel stressed or anxious. When a task is unfinished or interrupted, it causes what's known as The Zeigarnik Effect,[26] or "open loops" in the mind. Discovered in 1927 by Russian psychologist Dr. Bluma Zeigarnik, her research suggests that people remember these uncompleted tasks better than they do completed ones. These open loops distract us from tasks we are currently working on, reducing productivity and draining our mental energy. In essence, our mind can't rest until we close the loop. Over time, half-finished tasks lead to chaos and clutter, and a whole lot of stress.

If "Grouping Like with Like" is the helping principle then "Finish The Task" is, well, the finishing principle! It makes a huge difference when it comes to maintaining success with your organizing systems. In fact, even those who have mastered our other principles have gotten thrown off track when they've ignored this one. When you don't "finish the task," you increase the risk of creating more clutter and, ultimately, more work for yourself.

For example, if you are doing laundry, this task isn't complete until you have folded the clean laundry and put it away in your drawers and closet. Laundry left in the basket, even if it's clean and folded, is not done.

Let's explore how finishing (or not finishing) the task might impact this routine chore. You do a load of laundry and take the time to fold it nicely. You put it in a basket and carry it upstairs from your basement laundry room to your bedroom. You think to yourself, "Great, that's done. I'll put these clothes away later." You mentally check it off your list because you are super busy and you move on to your next task.

In the meanwhile, your daughter walks by your room, sees the basket and rummages through it to see if her favorite shirt is in there. It isn't, so she walks away. Now, many of the items in the basket are no longer folded nicely. In fact, it wouldn't be very clear whether these clothes are clean or dirty unless a person looked very closely. A little later, your son passes the room and thinks you are gathering dirty laundry to wash and dumps a whole bunch of his things in the basket. He's even thoughtful enough to carry it down to the laundry room for you.

Now you have clean laundry back downstairs in the laundry room! It's no longer folded nicely, so by the time you realize what's happened, some of it is wrinkled and will have to be ironed. At the very least, it will need to be refolded and brought back upstairs. Again.

What's more, you are now frustrated with your kids and tired at the thought that you have to redo something that you thought was done. Even if you make the kids take responsibility, there is now negative energy surrounding all of you.

Are you thinking this story is unrealistic? We assure you this scenario happens all too often and can be prevented simply by finishing the task. If you put the laundry away right after folding it, the rest of the above story will not happen.

There are variations of this story, too. Perhaps you live alone and don't have kids rummaging through your basket. Maybe you just leave the basket in your room and it sits there for days. You're stressed and busy and there are other more important things taking up your time. Instead of putting the clothes away, you start using your basket as an actual drawer and just get dressed out of the basket each day. It's in the way and doesn't look nice, but you push it around as necessary so you can get to other things in the room. After a while, this becomes normal and also annoying. You start to feel stressed whenever you enter your room.

The few minutes you save by not finishing the task in the moment will almost always cost you time in the end. This is another statement that bears repeating: *The few minutes you save by not finishing the task in the moment will almost always cost you time in the end.* It will also cause unnecessary frustration and stress.

We see this often with bill paying, although in today's day and age, more and more people are eliminating paper and handling things online. But for those who still like paper statements to keep track of what's due, not finishing the task can become a real hassle. For this group, bill paying is not complete until the statements are marked "paid" with the date and method of payment, and then filed away. If you don't keep your paid statements, then for you bill paying is not complete until you have shred or tossed the physical papers.

If you pay your bills online or by phone and leave the statements lying around, those statements are now clutter. Worse, if you haven't marked them paid and they sit around long enough, they will eventually get mixed in with more recent statements and you will wind up spending precious time figuring out what has been paid and what is still due. When life gets busy and too many months pass like this, you run the risk of missing payments and incurring late fees, all while surrounded by a growing pile of unsightly paper clutter. It is very easy to feel out of control when you don't have a handle on your financial record keeping. This can be solved by taking those few extra minutes to mark the statements "paid" and file them away, or toss/shred the statements so they are not still lying around.

While we are on the subject of bill-paying and paperwork, this very principle is one reason we are not fans of the "To File" file. You know, the one where you have looked at a piece of paper, determined you do need to keep it, so you place it in a folder marked "To File." If you stop there, you haven't truly finished the task. You still need to file it away in your long-term filing.

A pile of paper in a folder is still . . . a pile of paper. Since the folder brings it together in a tidy way, it's easy for it to become an "out of sight, out of mind" situation, a.k.a. an unfinished task. Until it actually gets filed, it becomes a little something we call "clutter." Tidy does not always mean organized and "task completed." When it comes to mail and paper, finishing the task means taking what no longer needs to be addressed and doing something with it to get it out of your main space.

Scenario: You look at a bank statement that comes in the mail and you don't need to take any further action. No calls need to be made. No transactions need to be addressed. It's just your regular monthly statement.

Two possible courses of action:

- You wish to keep the paper statement for reference. This should be filed away in your long-term filing. It should not float around on your kitchen counter, coffee table, floor, etc.

- You like physically receiving the monthly statement because otherwise you'd forget to check it online each month. However, after reviewing it, you don't feel the need to keep the paper statement. You can always access it online and you hate filing. Therefore, discard or shred it as soon as you're done reviewing it.

No matter what your preference is regarding keeping or discarding paperwork, one thing remains the same—the statement that you've reviewed no longer needs to stay in your main space. An additional action (filing/discarding/shredding) is needed to finish the task and prevent that piece of paper from 1) becoming clutter, and 2) getting mixed in with more recent paperwork.

The importance of unpacking

Finishing the task does not just relate to laundry and paperwork. It can be any situation where not seeing it through to the end will impact how smoothly your household runs and how uncluttered your space remains.

Take grocery shopping for example. Finishing the task means unpacking the supermarket bags and putting things in your cabinets, closets, or pantry according to the way you've set up your space (see chapter 10). Leaving things in the grocery bags not only looks unsightly, but also makes them more difficult to find and access. It also makes it harder to monitor expiration dates when some things are unpacked and others aren't.

And speaking of unpacking, let's talk about [cue menacing music]: *The Mystery Bag*. You know, the one shoved in the bottom of your closet that contains . . . oh, that's right! You have no idea what it contains because you can't see through it, and don't remember what was in it. Could it be those new clothes that you want to return? Or a mish-mosh of things you scooped up from the dining room table in a moment of panic when company unexpectedly arrived? These bags can get "lost" for weeks, months, even years. Mystery bags are not exotic and fun. They cause chaos.

If you buy stuff, finish the "shopping" task by taking it out of the bag and putting it away. If you have a return, finish the "purchase decision" task by putting it in your car and actually returning it. Unexpected company? Fine, shove everything on your dining room table in a bag and stick it in the closet (yeah, we said it). However, the moment they leave, take it all out again and finish the "straightening up" task by putting it all away in their proper homes (which is probably *not* on the dining room table!). We'd like to respectfully point out that finishing the task in the first place means that when company unexpectedly comes over, there won't be a mish-mosh of things on the dining room table.

Putting things away

Throughout the course of the day, as you and your family go about your activities, there may be lots of things temporarily out of place. For homes with multiple floors, it might not be practical to run up and down the stairs every single time something needs to be returned. Annmarie encountered this when she bought her first home years ago. She had lived in an apartment her whole life. Putting things away had been easy—all the rooms were close to each other! But in her house, putting things away became its own exercise routine. Talk about adding to your step count!

It became a habit to leave items that needed to go back upstairs or downstairs *on* the steps themselves. The idea was that the next time someone went upstairs, they would take what needed to go up and return it. The next time someone was going downstairs, they would do the same. It was meant to save time and energy by reducing the number of trips up and down. This is a perfectly reasonable system as long as everyone actually follows it. Otherwise, what do you have? A pile of clutter on the steps resulting from not finishing the task.

This was the case for many of our clients who also used the stairs this way. It must have been the case for a lot of families, because companies started selling these oddly shaped wicker baskets designed to sit on the stairs. It looked like an upside down "L" and was meant to corral things that needed to be returned to different floors. It had handles, so you could just grab it and go. It was supposed to make your pile of temporary clutter look less unsightly. More importantly, it was meant to make it easier to "finish the task" of putting things back in their homes. For some families, it worked. For many others, it backfired. Annmarie's was one such family:

*The basket made the pile look so neat and tidy that it became the visual equivalent of "white noise"—we didn't even notice it as we went up and down. Nothing looked messy, so the pile of clutter didn't "annoy us" into taking care of it, at least not until the basket itself could no longer hold any additional items and started to overflow. In fact, this organizing product reinforced behavior that made us **less** organized! Things weren't returned to their homes in a timely way so we couldn't find them the next time we needed them. We would forget that we had put them in the basket or didn't realize another family member had done so. These items would literally be lost in plain sight.*

This is a great example of how organizing systems have to work for you and your family. There could be a great system or product that works beautifully for others but doesn't work at all for you. This doesn't mean it's not a good product. That's why organizing is trial and error. There is more than one way to approach a challenge. However, all approaches should involve finishing the task. If your family is going to use the stairs as a temporary holding spot for things that need to be put away, be sure to grab a few things on the steps the next time you need to go up or down. Don't just bring them to the appropriate floor. Put them away immediately to finish the task! This way, they are available the next time you or someone else in the family goes to grab them. Remember, if you follow all of our principles, the items you are returning will all have specific homes, and everyone in the house will have an association of where those items "live." The longer they stay on the stairs, the greater the probability that they will wind up somewhere else.

Other ways to finish the task

Back in chapter 7, we suggested calling for a donation pickup before starting a decluttering project. Believe it or not, this can actually be considered a "Finish the Task" tip, too. As we discussed, it isn't enough to decide to donate something. The real triumph is actually getting it out of your home once the decision has been made. Once you've decided you no longer want/ need to keep something, it becomes clutter if it's just hanging around homeless. Not only does a scheduled donation pickup act as a motivating force to start your decluttering project, but also helps you finish the task of seeing your decisions through. The same goes for giving your things to family and friends— once you make the decision, commit to a pick-up or drop-off date and don't let the bags sit in limbo.

Many years ago, the advice columnist Ann Landers printed a poem called "Golden Rules for Living" by Miriam Hamilton Keare:[27]

1. If you open it, close it.
2. If you turn it on, turn it off.
3. If you unlock it, lock it up.
4. If you break it, admit it.

5. If you can't fix it, call in someone who can.
6. If you borrow it, return it.
7. If you value it, take care of it.
8. If you make a mess, clean it up.
9. If you move it, put it back.
10. If it belongs to someone else, get permission to use it.
11. If you don't know how to operate it, leave it alone.
12. If it's none of your business, don't ask questions.

While they are all wonderful rules for any family to live by, look at numbers 1, 2, 3, 6, 8, and 9—they are all "finish the task" rules!

1. If you open it, close it.
2. If you turn it on, turn it off.
3. If you unlock it, lock it up.
6. If you borrow it, return it.
8. If you make a mess, clean it up.
9. If you move it, put it back.

So simple, and yet so integral to keeping order and peace in the home! Really, these are basic rules of respect, and what a wonderful mindset to hold regarding your space and your things. What if we simply just treated them with the respect they deserve?

Numbers eight and nine remind us of this girl Meg when she was in high school. If Meg tried ten outfits on for school in the morning, nine of them would still be on the floor days later. While you wrap your head around the idea of trying on ten outfits each morning, let us explain.

Every morning, Meg made a mess in her room, similar to a tornado blasting through an unlucky town. She moved her clothes and accessories out of their "homes" and ultimately onto the floor, bed, and every other nearby surface, where they remained for days at a time. Inevitably, her clean clothes would become wrinkled or she wouldn't be able to find things she needed. Meg's parents would express their aggravation. This, in turn, would stress Meg out and put her in a bad mood. What if she had just finished the "deciding on a school outfit" task by putting away the pieces that didn't make the cut?

Keep in mind the expectation is not for Meg to have done it at that moment when she was rushing to get to school, or even immediately when she arrived home. However, what if she had finished the task and put her things away within a reasonable timeframe, say before bedtime? Her room wouldn't have looked like a disaster zone. Her other outfits would have been easy to find when she did want to wear them. Plus, they wouldn't have gotten wrinkled from being tossed all over. Her parents wouldn't have been aggravated, and no cross words would have been uttered. Meg wouldn't have gotten stressed out and would have started each day in a much better frame of mind. Finishing the task can be the difference between a positive spiral and a negative spiral.

How finishing the task affects your time

This principle doesn't just relate to clutter either. It helps with time management, too, particularly when it comes to daily life. For example, we suggest that whenever possible, avoid going to sleep with dishes in the sink. It's not that it would be the end of the world if you did. It's that you would be starting the next day already behind, which could affect your schedule, state of mind, and level of productivity (not to mention anxiety).

From a "Finish the Task" perspective, dinner is not over until the dishes are washed or loaded in the dishwasher and your counters are clean. In the morning you start fresh. The goal is to focus on the day ahead, not play catch-up from the day before. You will be a lot more productive if you begin each day with a clean slate. You will also be operating from a more focused, forward-thinking mindset. This carries a much different energy than starting the day with the feeling of being behind in your to-do list before you even get started.

In terms of time, you don't want to lose time today finishing tasks from yesterday. An emergency notwithstanding, why would you start today with yesterday's dishes in the sink?

Clutter accumulates from not finishing tasks: not putting things away, not addressing paperwork properly, not completing household chores. Eventually, things will get to the point where you are forced to address it, and this will almost always take longer than if you had just finished these tasks at the time. One unfinished task may not have an impact, but many unfinished tasks in the same time period can add up to hours of straightening up or flat-out reorganizing later on.

Interestingly, just as finishing the task helps with time management, good time management can support you in consistently finishing your tasks. Time management skills can be easily learned and developed.

The key is to plan ahead and be proactive rather than reactive.

Set aside time to do a particular project like you would set an appointment for a routine doctor visit or exercise class at the gym. It is not uncommon to underestimate the amount of time you will need to complete a project. In the beginning, we recommend doubling or even tripling how long you think it will take. If you don't have that much time available to allocate, start out smaller. For example, if you plan to tackle your kitchen or home office and don't have enough time to do the whole room, schedule enough time to tackle one small drawer. This way you can see this smaller project through to the end, thereby finishing the task! This will give you a sense of accomplishment and inspire you to keep going!

There will be times that despite your best efforts, you will have to temporarily stop working on a project before it is complete. Life happens. Ideally, you want to set another "appointment" to finish as soon as possible. Saying it is "almost finished" does not carry the same weight as saying it *is* finished." Write a note to indicate today's date, where you left off, and what still needs to be done. You can write it in your planner or use the notes app on your phone. When you start up again, you just quickly refamiliarize yourself with what needs to be done and dig right in.

Why labeling is necessary

Perhaps the ultimate expression of finishing the task is the strategy of labeling. Establishing a home for your things is super important, and taking the time to label your bins, shelving units, and drawers just increases your chances of organizing success significantly. Even when you have things in clear containers and can easily see what's inside, finishing the organizing task with labeling benefits you in several ways:

- It reinforces the category that is contained in that space, strengthening your association of where it is located.
- Seeing the label will deter you from shoving something that doesn't belong in there, even when you are in a rush.
- It takes all the think-work out of finding what you need, making it very quick and easy to do so without expending unnecessary time and energy.

Of course, the labels will only be effective if you respect them! Once you dump something in a bin or space that is labeled for another category, the organizing system will start to unravel.

The labels are there to make it easier for you to finish the task, so be sure to let them do their job!

Why this principle is important
Finishing the Task:

- Is the secret weapon for maintaining the integrity and efficacy of your organizing systems.
- Prevents clutter by addressing where things go immediately.
- Reduces the chances of having to do double work.
- Helps to reduce stress and anxiety and increase productivity.

What mastering this principle will save you
Time: Finishing a task will always save you time in the end because you are completing it while you have momentum. When unfinished tasks add up, it takes time to figure out what's what and then complete them.

Money: This principle saves money in indirect ways. In terms of bill paying, addressing paperwork in a timely fashion reduces the accrual of interest charges and late fees. When it comes to laundry, not having to rewash items saves money on water and detergent. Unpacking groceries helps with the monitoring of expiration dates, reducing the chances that things will go bad. Remembering to put returns in the car (and then actually returning them) means getting money back for items you have determined you don't want or need.

Energy: Finishing the task means less energy spent redoing a task or readdressing a situation. It also means less frustration and fewer negative emotions, which quickly deplete our energy.[28] Labeling bins, closets, and shelves takes 100 percent of the guesswork out of what should go in a particular space. This saves mental energy, leaving you extra for more critical decision making.

Space: Finishing the task means way less clutter. Enough said.

PART III

PUTTING IT ALL TOGETHER

CHAPTER 12

How to Create Effective Organizing Systems

Now, be honest. Did you read the other chapters or did you jump right to this one in the hope of cutting to the chase? We know how tempting it must seem, especially since you're probably super anxious to learn how to put it all together. However, the real meat of this sandwich lies in what came before now. If you haven't already done so, we strongly encourage you to go back and read each of the other chapters. There is a wealth of information to be learned!

For those who have already done this, let's dive in. To recap, our top eight organizing principles are:

1. Goal Setting and Other Tools for Your Organizing Toolbox
2. Have a Vision for Each Space and Establish Clear Zones
3. Sort Through Your Belongings and Group "Like with Like"

4. Decide What Stays and What Goes
5. Everything Deserves a Home
6. Create Associations Between Your Things and Where They Live
7. Manage Your Space (So You Can Manage Your Inventory)
8. Finish the Task!

Each principle we've shared has its own unique value. Mastering any one of them will automatically up your organizing game. They all strengthen your awareness and intention about your space and belongings in some way. They increase confidence by helping you avoid energy depletion, giving you more mental resources to stay consistent with your organizing routine. They each play a part in helping you feel more in control of your life.

Can you be organized without using every principle? Yes. However, employing all of them will fast-track your progress and give you the best results possible. It will also increase your chances of staying on track, because you know the all-important "why" behind each step. Beyond achieving short-term project "wins," organizing will become an integral part of who you are and how you approach the different areas of your life.

And that, friends, is when organizing goes from efficient to life-changing.

For the chronically disorganized person, our principles will lay a very important foundation for learning the skills needed to live a more organized life. The transformation will not happen overnight, but that's to be expected! The disorganization and clutter didn't happen overnight either. It will, however, build over time with consistent commitment, effort, and patience.

For the person who is already somewhat organized, our principles can take what is working well and elevate it to the next level. Back in the introduction, we spoke about the real definition of being organized. You may remember that the first example was "knowing what you have and where to find it when you need it." We've seen homes where things seem visibly cluttered, but the homeowner actually has a good grip on what they have. Believe it or not, they are organized to a certain degree even though their photos will never make it to Pinterest.

In this case, the goal would be to *build on the foundation they've already created*. What is working? What isn't? What roadblocks do they encounter? If a person already keeps a category of items in a certain location, the next step might be to help them manage that space more effectively (Manage Your Space So You Can Manage Your Inventory). This might mean purging down their inventory to include only what is truly needed (Sort Through Your Belongings/Group Like with Like and Decide What Stays and What Goes)

Maybe it means rethinking how they place things on a shelf or in a drawer. Maybe it's trying our tip for using clear bins to create "drawers" on a shelf in their pantry (Manage Your Space So You Can Manage Your Inventory). Maybe it's going back to the beginning and really honing in on what they want a particular space to be (Have a Vision for Each Space and Establish Clear Zones).

In other words, by learning and mastering these principles, you will now have an arsenal of tools in your toolbox for improving the way things look and function. Here are some other concepts to consider when creating organizing systems for your family:

1. Choose What Works for You

Even though we have great systems that work for us, we are constantly learning from others and trying new things. Sometimes they work and other times they don't. The important thing is to find what works for you and your family. If at first you don't succeed, don't quit! Try again and again until you hit upon the system that encourages consistently positive behavior. A perfectly good system for one person might be a terrible choice for someone else. It doesn't mean it's not a good system. It's just not the right system for *you*. If it's not the right system for you, the likelihood of you sticking with it is significantly reduced.

Here's a blog post Annmarie wrote on the subject:

Confessions of an Organizer: I used to stink at taking my vitamins.

Yeah, I know. Not a very exciting confession, but let's face it. My exciting confessions are not going to end up in a blog about organizing ;). My vitamin story, however, does help illustrate an important point: An organizing strategy or product is only good if it works for you. If it doesn't, don't use it, even if it works great for other people. Here's my story:

Once upon a time, I wasn't taking my vitamins on a regular basis and I didn't feel great. I also heard rumors that I was moody, but those people are liars so, you know, whatever. . . . Anyway, I had tried several really good suggestions on how to remember, but most of them just didn't work for me. Doesn't mean they weren't good organizing tools/products/tips. They just didn't work for *me*. First, I tried keeping the bottles out on the counter. Makes sense, right? I figured if I saw them every day, it would be an instant reminder! But it really annoyed me seeing them every day. I mean, it reeeeaaaallllly annoyed me. Many times, I would notice them as I was running out the door and wasn't willing to make the time to open seven bottles. So, day after day, no vitamins.

Then I tried our own tip, which was to use one of those handy-dandy seven-day pill organizers. These work like a charm for so many of my friends (including Marie, my partner in crime!); I still stand by them and would recommend them to our clients. But they didn't work for me. Again, a lot of times I would remember to take my vitamins as I was leaving the house and didn't feel like schlepping the whole seven-day supply with me. I would convince myself that I would take them later, and then never did.

Next, I got fancy. I bought one of those new-fangled seven-day organizers with detachable compartments. That's *right, folks, I wasn't messing around. Guess what? I hated them. I could detach them ok, but I found it frustrating and difficult to reattach them, and I just couldn't be bothered (Translation: I wanted to fling them against the wall and/or crush them. Often.)*

So what finally worked? A month's supply of individual, disposable pill pouches that I found right at the drugstore. I fill them at the beginning of each month.

To some, this would seem like a crazy amount of work. But the point is . . . drum roll please . . . it works for me. It only takes about ten minutes once a month. Approximately twenty-nine days out of the month, I don't have to open seven bottles, and I don't have to see them on the counter, either. I just grab and go, and I'm healthier for it. As with any organizing challenge, don't quit if the first try doesn't work out. Keep at it until you find what works for you.

Gotta go . . . take my vitamins.

When trying out a new system or product, please allow a reasonable amount of time to really see if it works or doesn't. Don't make the decision after just one day. "Live" with it a bit and allow yourself to adjust to the change. If it doesn't work, that's okay. You can tweak the system or try another product.

2. Know Thyself

In figuring out how to best manage your time, space, belongings, and paperwork, it's important to have self-awareness about what actions you are willing to take. Notice we didn't say "capable of taking." We said "willing to take." That's because we truly believe, with the exception of physical restrictions due to injury or illness, you are capable of following through on most tasks. This does not mean you are willing or likely to do them.

For example, to hide or not to hide? That is the question. Some of our clients do not wish to see anything on their kitchen counters or desktops and ask us to design organizing systems where everything is behind a door or in a drawer. From an aesthetic standpoint, it makes them feel calmer when there is less to look at. We completely understand this mindset.

However, if out of sight means out of mind, this may not be the best approach in terms of practicality and productivity. In this case, we would recommend a different type of system and explain our reasons why.

For example, every household has daily mail and paperwork. Placing it all in a "to do" folder in a file cabinet out of sight will only work if you are diligent about taking that folder out and addressing it every single day. If you are, then keeping the folder out of sight will be perfectly fine. It will make your counters and other surfaces look less cluttered and will not affect your productivity. If not, then you are setting yourself up to fail. Even though your room will look less cluttered, you will technically be less organized because this system is hiding the clutter so well that you are forgetting about the paperwork and consequently not keeping up with it.

Know thyself. In the beginning, the goal is to establish positive organizing behaviors. This takes time. If your reality is you won't think to look in the cabinet every day because life is super busy, then hiding the unaddressed mail and paperwork in a cabinet won't serve your *initial* goal of getting a grip on it. In fact, this would be one of those situations where being too tidy actually hinders the organizing process.

As a compromise, we may ask you to consider a desktop organizer with open compartments wide enough to hold file folders. This would allow you to separate out your paperwork by type (yes, "Grouping Like with Like"!) and still have it be very visible and accessible. Consequently, it would be more likely to get handled. Once it is, it can then be filed completely out of sight wherever you keep your long-term filing. You would create this association: The home for incoming mail and unaddressed paperwork is the desktop organizer. Once you address something in it, you can then "Finish the Task" and file it away in long-term filing (its permanent home).

Here's another "know thyself" example: For some, if the organizing bin has a lid, they are not going to open it to put things away. It's actually fascinating to witness. We've seen dirty clothes on top of hampers, even though it would have taken a second to lift the lid and put them inside. We've seen houses with lidded file boxes with the filing sitting on top of the lid. The irony is that the homeowners bought these items with lids because they didn't want to see clutter. They wanted to hide it. Yet the lid itself was the barrier to them seeing that action through. *Now* there was clutter on top of organizers and behaviorally, they were avoiding good habits that would have kept things organized.

Know thyself. If this sounds like you, choose organizing products without lids, at least until you establish a very strong habit of putting your things away. When a task is considered undesirable, the best way to ensure success is to make it as easy as possible to get it done. You don't want to give yourself any reason or excuse not to do it. If the lids on organizing products are a barrier—literally and figuratively—avoid them. Would it be nice if the dirty laundry or filing wasn't visible? Sure. But know thyself. If having the lid means you dump stuff on top of the organizer, that's even less attractive. Keep the receptacles open and make it as easy as possible to put things inside. Once you have established this behavior, then try lids again and see if you can stay consistent.

On the other hand, there are those who never met a surface or an open receptacle they didn't like. If there is an empty place to dump something in the moment, they will do so. It is particularly important for this group to have a specific home for everything, to intentionally create strong associations about where things live, and finish the task. These folks may wish to have lids on their containers with very visible labeling so they take that extra pause before dumping. The pause will give them time to think about what their next action will be, and remind them that dumping now will only cost them time and energy in the long run. In this case, the label is also acting as a "primer," one of the organizing tools we introduced in chapter 4. Hopefully, this will prompt them to make a choice that supports the organized life they are trying to create.

If you hate filing so much that the very idea of it makes you sick to your stomach, it would not be in your best interest to design an intricate and involved filing system. It doesn't matter how pretty it looks or that it's color coded and "should be" easy to follow. If it's a big "to do" you are going to avoid doing it. You will be better off designing the simplest system possible—one that can be maintained quickly and with a minimum amount of effort.

This is especially true if you are just starting out. The process of getting organized involves behavior change and good habit development. These take time to establish, and if you try to change too much at once, you will get burnt out. Which bring us to our next concept:

3. Keep it Simple, Silly! (a.k.a. The "KISS" Method)

What's the extreme opposite of a disorganized person? The Over-Organizer! This person has a label maker and is *not* afraid to use it! Is this you? While we admire your enthusiasm, we also want to be sure that you are not setting yourself (and your spouse and children) up to fail. Don't create so many different categories and labels that you make it impossible to follow through.

Years ago, one of our clients made a very sincere effort to get more organized so she could better manage her household. She had health challenges that made it difficult to keep up with everyday tasks. She thought if she labeled everything, it would help her and her family remember where everything goes. Of course, that's a great line of thinking! She got off track when she became too specific in her labeling, creating an instant problem every time something didn't fit the label exactly. This caused stress and real feelings of defeat, which only depleted her energy even more. She found great relief when we taught her to choose a different type of organizing product and label a little more broadly. More on this a little later in the chapter. Right now, let's continue to talk about keeping things simple.

Every year we are asked about a good filing system, and people are always surprised by what we tell them. For those who are "file challenged," or who have never filed in their lives, keep it simple.

Try our super-easy filing system: Take twelve file folders and label them by month (month only, not the year). When something is ready to be filed (the bill has been paid; the statement has been reviewed, etc.), place it right in the folder for that particular month. Don't separate everything out; if it relates to a particular month, place it in the folder. This may seem counterintuitive—didn't we just teach you to sort and group "like with like?" Yes, and we still want you to do that! However, at this point in the process, "Grouping Like with Like" means grouping together all paperwork that pertains to the same month. Remember that *your initial goal is just to get used to filing.*

In sorting by month rather than individual company names, you will have fewer folders to manage, making it easier to establish good filing habits. When it comes to paid bills, you can choose to file them according to the month the payment is due or the month in which you actually paid them. Ideally, the month would be the same for both, but this is not always the case. Happily, getting more organized with paperwork can support timelier bill paying, help you avoid late fees, and increase your credit score. Win. Win. Win!

Are there exceptions to the monthly files? Yes—contracts that span multiple years, such as your mortgage or rental agreement, health and medical records, and any other category your family wishes to keep separate. Other than these, try this simple system if you are currently drowning in paperwork and wish to dig out from under. If you need to find something, everything is contained and your worst-case scenario is searching through twelve folders. Better than searching piles and piles throughout your whole house! At the end of the year, take the contents of the twelve folders and consolidate them into one folder marked by the year. Then you can reuse the monthly folders. It's not fancy, color-coded or complicated—just manageable.

Of course, if your paper management skills are a little more advanced, there are still ways to simplify in order to make filing less tedious. Consolidate files by category instead of having a single folder for each individual company. For example, your categories might include utility bills, health/medical, banking, credit cards etc.

Believe it or not, even though Annmarie is not at all "file challenged," she herself uses the super-easy filing system. She simply dislikes filing and would rather spend her time and energy doing something else. She "knows herself" and her husband. This system works for them, so despite being able to manage a "fancy shmancy" and far more complicated system, she just doesn't want to. She keeps it simple! Sometimes, the simplest solutions are the most effective.

4. Choose and Use the Right Products

Nowadays there is an abundance of organizing products out there, in every shape, color, and price point. A trip to the home improvement store can be both exhilarating and overwhelming. We are often asked about our favorite organizing products, but right now we'd like you to think more broadly in terms of what to consider when making purchase decisions:

- **Square/Rectangular versus Round**
  Two words: Right angles! Ninety-nine percent of the time, we recommend that clients purchase organizers that are cubic or rectangular versus round. That's because when you place them side by side in a drawer or cabinet, they fit snugly. This ensures no precious storage space is lost. Round organizers may look aesthetically pleasing but they aren't practical. When you place them next to each other, you lose the space in between the organizers where they curve.

Right angles also give you more storage room *inside* the organizer itself. For example, when you look at the sides of a cubic or rectangular storage bin, they are perpendicular to the base. Avoid organizers with slanted sides. The tops and bottoms of these organizers differ in size, making it challenging to store things nicely. The base *should be the same size* as the opening at the top. This gives you more useable space, and also more options for storing things inside, whether laying items flat or placing them vertically. (By the way, this is a great story to tell when your kids ask when they are *ever* going to need geometry in everyday life!)

- **Horizontal versus Vertical**
  While tall, vertical organizers are good for things like baseball bats and lacrosse sticks, they present a challenge for many other types of items. Tall units often create an "abyss"—a place where things enter but are never seen again. Shallower, horizontal bins make it less likely that things will get lost on the bottom.

  If you have a vertical organizer and you wish to avoid buying anything new, use it for taller items, such as the sports equipment we mentioned before, wrapping paper rolls, or longer umbrellas.

  A word about toy chests: While they are horizontal, they have the same risks associated with them. They look so pretty, and we often associate them with the perfect nursery or child's room. However, the deep storage space that toy chests provide often causes them to become "catchalls." Looking for a quick clean up? Throw it in the toy chest.

The problem is that smaller items get lost in the abyss, just like they do with vertical organizers. Furthermore, kids tend to play with only what's on top and easily accessible. If you have one, or feel you must get one, designate a very specific purpose for it, such as dress-up clothing or balls. Whatever it is, it should all be the same and the toy chest should only be used for that category.

- **Clear versus Solid**
We are happy to say there is a place for both in an organized home! Having opaque organizers allows you to align the organization with your décor, especially when what you are storing must be in plain sight.

When this is not the case, we do recommend clear bins and organizers. They have a clean look, and it is easier to see what is inside. Still, we strongly recommend labeling all bins, even clear ones. One of the main goals of getting organized is not wasting any time looking for things you need. Seeing the label takes 100 percent of the guesswork out of it. Having a label also makes it as easy as possible to "finish the task" and put things back where they belong. Hopefully, it will deter you and your family from just throwing something in a bin that

doesn't belong just to get it out of sight. We always tell
our clients to "respect the label!"

- **Color Coding**

Ever notice that whenever Halloween rolls around, you
start to see orange storage bins in the stores? Color
coding is a great organizational tool. By using orange
bins for autumn/Halloween, red for Christmas, blue for
Hanukkah and so on, it's super easy to identify which
decorations you need to get out of storage when the time
comes.

You can use color coding for other things, too, like
your calendar, by assigning a different color for each
family member when writing down activities and
appointments. In a pinch, your eyes will be able to
quickly focus on the info you need, making it a snap to
figure out who needs to be where and when!

Color coding can also be a tool within the KISS
system! We have a client who owns and manages
multiple properties. This means multiple sets of
paperwork. He assigns different colored hanging folders
for each property (blue for his main residence, yellow for
his summer home, red and green for his investment
properties). All folders related to a particular location
are housed in the corresponding color. When he needs
to file or reference something, he goes directly to the
appropriately colored folder. Easy peasy.

One more note about choosing organizing products: be intentional about the type of product you purchase and what purpose it will serve. You will save a lot of time and money if you consider the points above before you buy. We're not saying that you can't try out different products. (We love a good trip to the Container Store®!) However, we want you to remember that *the organizing product is just a tool to support the inner work and planning that defines the organizing process*. It can't do the work for you or "make" you more organized. It's like a fancy treadmill you buy in order to lose weight. Unless you commit to a workout schedule and healthy eating plan, the treadmill will wind up becoming a lovely place to hang your dry cleaning.

Remember our label-happy client from earlier in the chapter? In addition to over-labeling, her husband was actually the manager of a home store who got a wonderful discount on merchandise. As such, he constantly brought home organizing products in an attempt to help his wife get things under control. The problem is they weren't the right products for their situation, needs, and family dynamic. A lot of them had too many little drawers and compartments, which for them wasn't a good fit. It was a lot like an episode of *Let's Make a Deal*. Finding what they needed was like having to guess what was behind door number one, two, or three. It even confused their kids! Their garage was literally filled with organizing products, yet they were completely disorganized when we first met them. More organizing products does not mean more *organized*! It was only after they learned our basic principles and understood what it truly means to be organized did they start choosing products that supported their needs.

5. Pave the Way for Your Children's Success

It's never too early to start training your younger kids to be organized, and it's never too late to teach an "older" dog (we mean kid) new tricks. As parents, we sometimes don't give our children enough credit and think they are incapable of putting their things away. Let's empower them by teaching them organizing skills they can apply to all areas of their lives. We promise they will thank you at some point, maybe even earlier than you think! That was the certainly the case with Marie's son:

When Nicolas was in 5th grade, I visited him at school for Parent Day. His workspace was nice and organized. Later that day, he mentioned how many of his classmates could never find anything easily, whether it be in school or at home. He thanked me for teaching him to be organized from a young age because it helped him to be focused and on top of his homework and studying, and to be a better student in general. He saw the difference in his behavior versus his classmates' and how they never seemed prepared. It was incredibly rewarding as both a parent and a professional organizer to hear these genuine words of gratitude from a ten-year-old. Fast forward to today: Nicolas is a sophomore in college now and still on top of his game. Organizing for the parenting win!

In addition to introducing your children to the principles in this book, the key to success with children is leading by example. One time, our client's six-year-old daughter observed us working and said, "I like to do things like mommy does them." Such an important example of how parents' behavior affects their children. They may not always listen, but they are *always watching*.

It's not reasonable to expect your kids to put their toys away if you don't do the same with your things. Your children take their cues from you, so designating a specific home for all your things, grouping like with like and putting things away (a.k.a. finishing the task) are just a few inspiring ways to lead by example.

Last but not least, don't forget to label! This is a great opportunity to employ the KISS Method. Even children who can't read yet can benefit from labels with pictures on them. Get them involved in the process by having them cut out pictures from magazines. Make a craft session out of it so they associate organizing and labeling with fun! For older kids, ask them what wording makes the most sense to them. We once made a label for a young girl who was very clear about what she was putting in the bin—hair clips that open and close like a clamp. So "Clampy Clips" it was! Perfectly simple, and perfectly effective. The more invested your children are, the more likely they will be to follow through with returning things to their proper "homes." And that's a win for everyone!

CHAPTER 13

Reflections

When we first started our business thirteen years ago, we had a simple mission: to help other people discover what we had—that an organized home makes it easier and less stressful to get through day-to-day life. We had gone through a life transition (having kids) that had taken us out of our comfort zone. Transitioning to parenthood was one big emotional roller coaster. While we truly did feel joy, wonder, amazement, and hope, we also felt frustration, stress, and anxiety. Like many new parents, there were days when we felt flat-out inept! It didn't matter that we weren't *actually* inept. The power of negative thinking coupled with hormones and emotions sometimes got the better of us. Looking back now, we understand that this is not unusual and is often temporary. But back then, it felt overwhelming.

When we were going through it, our only goal was to get a better handle on things and make the house *not* look like a scene from a war zone. Not too much to ask for, right? We knew we wanted to regain some control over our physical space and the things within it. We had no idea that getting organized would affect so many other areas of our lives.

As we started to make sense of our environment, other things made sense, too. When we felt that sense of mastery over our personal belongings, we felt calmer and less reactive. We enjoyed activities more. Our mood was more positive and steady. Our confidence grew. We felt . . . empowered.

We want you to feel empowered, too.

We'll circle back to what we said in the introduction: Organizing is not how "neat and tidy" something looks on the outside. Rather, it's how the set-up and layout of your drawers, cabinets, and closets *support the way you and your family want to live.* That may have sounded odd in the beginning—support the way my family and I want to live? What do my drawers have to do with that?

Hopefully, you now understand a basic truth:

Both organization and disorganization influence how we show up in the world.

Both affect confidence, reliability, trust, mood, and emotional regulation. Both affect how much quality time we have for the people and activities we love. They impact how we manage our money. They affect how other people perceive us. Both affect how much energy we spend, which in turn impacts how quickly we get depleted.

That's a lot of influence in your life, so which supports your dreams for you and your family—organization or disorganization?

We asked some of our clients to reflect back on their organizing journey with the following questions as a guide:

1. When you first called us, how was disorganization affecting your life?
2. What did you discover during the organizing process itself? (What connections did you make? What insightful moments did you have?)
3. What impact has becoming more organized had on your life, home, and family?

Here are some of their responses:

Basically, I didn't know where to start, so every time I thought about it, it was too much to tackle. It really was, but that feeling would then paralyze me and [I would] either do very little or nothing. I would then think I needed more [products] to organize my stuff. I struggled with getting help, because I was associating it with feeling incompetent. Why couldn't I just BE more organized like other people or how others expected me to be? Feeling disorganized made me feel almost incompetent and definitely frustrated at times, because I truly believed I should just know or have figured out what I needed and where everything should be.

I had many, many connections and insightful moments throughout my sessions. My biggest discovery was that I wasn't giving myself enough credit for what I did manage to do in my extremely busy schedule as a wife, mom, and full-time employee. Our conversations about "being organized" versus "being an organizer" helped me be at ease with the fact that it was okay not to be able to figure it all out on my own. I would compare myself with others and put myself down without knowing if they had help. Maybe others get their stuff organized, too. On how to integrate the kids, I learned precise labeling and techniques to keep them involved. Seeing how happy my six year old was to easily reach his shirts—he helped me hang them up and then on his own organized them by color—was truly mind blowing and something I was NOT expecting. Another huge aspect was poor time management. I would definitely attempt too much at once and would get so overwhelmed that I would not continue for weeks. The solution of setting pockets of time, actually using a timer, even in fifteen-minute increments, have allowed me to chip away at my bigger organization projects.

The fact that I got over my fear of asking for help was a huge deal! Yes, this is a service one pays for, but my main aspect was overcoming the FEAR behind needing help with ideas and tools. I constantly thought I should learn and do this on my own. I have been able to successfully maintain what was organized to better use my space (especially in my bedroom closet that was resembling more of a storage unit than a clothing closet.) As a result, I have worked towards upgrading my bedroom to ensure it is a more enjoyable and relaxing space. It all comes down to peace of mind and feeling more accomplished—definitely something that benefits any home or family. This investment has been priceless as I continue to apply what I've learned in other areas of the home. —Eunice

In the nine years after I retired, my accumulation of clutter had gotten out of hand. I realized that it had the potential to create a safety hazard. I think clutter is something you just manage to ignore—especially if you are able (as I was) to maintain a few areas that are always organized. (In my case these were a downstairs area for entertaining and my bedroom as well as both bathrooms.) Those uncluttered areas give one a kind of "oasis." Also, if you are able to find whatever you need, despite being in a cluttered area, you still feel reasonably organized (even while admitting that you are probably wasting time digging past other stuff in the process.) Although it was a potential safety issue that prompted me to directly address the clutter in my upstairs living room, honesty forces me to admit that there were times when I was a bit embarrassed if someone came to the front door and noticed the state of that room. I certainly didn't see myself as a "pack rat," but I wasn't comfortable with the idea that a stranger might gain that impression based on a glance into the house.

My big a-ha moment was in the realization that deferring decisions is dangerous because it tends to permit little tasks to pile up. Then you're faced with a BIG job of sorting and deciding all at once. It's just easier to avoid deferred decisions as much as possible. My resolve is not perfect, so now I have a couple of "fallback" provisions. One is to limit the amount of space allotted for papers, etc. requiring attention. (One box—and if it gets too full, then decisions MUST be made before anything else can be added.) Another is to establish periodic intervals for tidying up. (Every other Monday before the cleaning lady arrives on Tuesday.) [Another a-ha moment was] it can actually be fun to take on an "organizing" project. My most recent one was just re-organizing the four file drawers in my desk to reflect new priorities in my life. The result is a wonderful sense of satisfaction when things are "in order." Life is so much simpler when there's a dedicated space to put something whenever I handle it.

When I decided to relocate, which involved a certain amount of downsizing, the fact that my house was reasonably well-organized and I'd gotten rid of a lot of superfluous stuff certainly made my move much easier. As a corollary, I'm trying to become a little more selective about what I allow into my life. If there's less stuff to begin with, then it's so much easier to keep things organized and have a comfortable feeling of control over my life. —Ann

---

I could never find anything! I had a lot of unnecessary paperwork. We purged a lot of it. I was recently looking for very important papers and found exactly what I needed, instantly! It took away the stress of, "Where is it?"

I discovered that I had things just mixed up together with no rhyme or reason. We dumped things together any old way! Now we "group like things together" and I know where to find things or add things to areas that we've already organized.

It helps me save money. I used to buy things, then realize I already had one or two at home. I found money as well in the strangest places! The house is definitely neater, which is always a relief. I find it very stressful and I get anxiety when my house is out of control. Everything has a place. Labels help with the kids, to put things back where they belong. —Lisa

****

I had the unfortunate experience of discovering that my housekeeper of many years had been stealing items from me over an extended period of time. Most of what she took was clothing and small personal items. I came to realize that our disorganization and clutter enabled her to take advantage of our inability to quickly determine that something was, in fact, missing.

What was very eye opening for me was the psychology behind the organization process. Taking a look at all your stuff and having to make decisions on what to keep, what to throw away and what to donate is daunting! You made me take a hard look at what I was using—and NOT using. You looked at a room in a much more efficient way and helped me see it in a different/more logical way.

I became more efficient on my own and was able to easily continue what we set up. Of course, little tweaks here and there are sometimes necessary—life is always changing and adjustments usually need to be made from time to time. Having a more organized home makes life so much easier, and therefore happier. We live in such a fast-paced, distracted, multi-tasking world that it is necessary to be organized to be efficient or *simply get things done. I am much happier and much less stressed! —Maggie*

∞∞∞∞∞∞∞∞∞∞∞∞∞∞∞∞∞∞∞∞∞∞∞∞∞∞∞∞∞∞∞∞∞∞∞∞∞∞∞

When I first called you, disorganization affected me by creating frequent, stressful thoughts. My head would be filled with thoughts of needing to organize and not liking things the way they were. It made me feel unsettled and not in control. Not having things organized was like a burden and a constant annoyance. I wanted to organize and declutter but I felt stuck and needed help, support, and objective eyes.

Oh my goodness, I became more aware that I do not focus on one thing at a time. I realized I jump from thing to thing. My thoughts and ideas were all over the place in a frantic rush. This self-awareness was huge. I was operating like this all the time and not realizing it. I saw with (your) fresh eyes that there were better ways to arrange things that I never would have thought of. I learned how much labeling helps, and that it is so easy to straighten up if everything has a place where it belongs. Now, I love having things organized, and I am motivated to keep up with things every time I see my attic, shed, business, or craft materials. I also learned that organizing goes beyond decluttering and purging and that I should not feel guilty for wanting to keep certain things.

I feel so relaxed when I walk in my shed or go up to my attic. I save time. I know what I have. I now use methods and routines that keep me organized. I learned not to be so hard on myself. I buy less "things." Now, before I purchase something, I think about if I really want to bring it into my house and have it take up space and so I am saving money! I am a new business owner and never realized how much money I was investing and spending. I feel more at peace, more professional, and calmer in my office space. Also, I am aware when disorganization is starting and I take timely action so it does not become a problem again. —Janice

※※※※※※※※※※※※※※※※※※※※※

We hope that when you take some time to reflect on your own journey, you will choose Team Organization hands down.

Thank you from the bottom of our hearts for taking a chance on us and this book. It is our hope that after reading it, you will come away feeling like you have everything it takes to be an active creator, not only of your dream home, but of your dream life as well.

Dream big . . . and beyond tidy!
XO
Annmarie and Marie

Acknowledgments

As new authors, writing this book was as exhilarating as it was terrifying! We could not have done it without the generous help of so many.

To our husbands, Freddie and John-Paul, a.k.a. our unsuspecting guinea pigs. Over the years, you've given us a truckload of teaching and social media material just by being your stubborn selves. Yet, you've *always* acknowledged us when our tried and true organizing tips proved to be the bomb. Thank you for believing in us and supporting us as we shifted from Corporate America to the uncharted waters of entrepreneurship. Creating this book took many hours away from family time, and we appreciate you allowing us to go out and play. We love you with all our hearts.

To our beautiful children, Daniella, Nicolas, and Julianna, whose entrance into this world sparked the transition that has led us here. We started our company to do something meaningful while still giving us the freedom to pick you up from school each day. Despite testing many of the principles in this book, as well as our patience, you remain our greatest joy and finest achievements! We are filled with enormous pride, and love you to infinity. It's humbling to watch how organization has positively influenced the way in which you navigate the world.

To our girls, Allie Dineson, Colleen Pelar, Janice Imbrogno, Maura Messina, and Maureen Szabo, who read the rough manuscript and gave us loving, productive and honest feedback. We can't thank you enough for sharing your time and expertise with us. We are so grateful for your friendship and support.

To our extended family and friends—your excitement and love from the moment we started our business have meant the world to us. We are equally grateful for your support throughout this new chapter of becoming authors. Whether it was a hot meal so we could continue writing, an encouraging word, a curious question or just your positive energy—you are the fuel that kept us going. You are the fuel that *always* keeps us going. We love you more than words can say.

To our current and former clients, who by allowing us into their homes gave us the platform to create the material in this book. Thank you for trusting us with your stories, your homes, your families and your vulnerability. We have never taken that for granted, not even for a moment. We are humbled by your faith in us, and we continue to support and celebrate you!

A special thank you to Ann, Eunice, Janice, Lisa, and Maggie who graciously shared their stories for our final chapter. We appreciate how deeply you reflected upon the ways in which your life has been impacted by our journey together. Thank you for your generosity of time and insight. We love when you tell us we're "in your head," and also, we apologize . . . but not really.

Another very special thank you to Jackie and Jennifer for allowing us to use their photos and project details in our case studies chapter. Your generosity will inspire so many people by (literally) helping them "see" what's possible!

To our editor, Jesse McHugh, and the entire team at Skyhorse Publishing for making our maiden voyage to authorhood a wonderful experience. Thank you for treating us with respect and educating us on the many steps that go into creating a non-fiction book. We appreciate your warm welcome, patience, and dedication to creating a quality product for the reader.

We would like to make special mention of Jason Schneider at Skyhorse, without whom we would not have had this opportunity. Thank you for reaching out to us and for your openness to new ideas. We only wish you could have stayed long enough to meet us in person and see this dream come to fruition. May you rest in eternal peace.

To Thomas Hanna, our publishing attorney, for his professionalism and expertise. We appreciate the time you took to answer our many questions, and for your excellent follow-up. Thank you for making the legal aspects of publishing easy to understand, and much less overwhelming.

To all the positive psychology researchers whose work not only inspires us, but gives us the science and the language to support the concepts we have been teaching all along. We are grateful for your passion and dedication to helping people lead happy, flourishing lives. A special thank you to Emiliya

Zhivotovskaya of The Flourishing Center in New York City, for your support and assistance in citing the important research contained in this book, and for so much more.

Last but certainly not least, many thanks to our fellow professional organizers. All of us have a unique way of connecting with our clients and sharing our knowledge. Each organizer may approach things differently, but our collective goal is always to inspire others and empower them to move forward. We are pleased to be in such good company and wish you all continued success!

About the Authors

Annmarie Brogan is a professional organizer and co-owner of Organize Me! of NY, LLC. She is also a certified positive psychology-based life coach and resilience trainer. Prior to becoming a professional organizer, Annmarie had a successful corporate career in magazine publishing, advertising and qualitative market research. She lives on Long Island with her husband, daughter and 12-year-old "puppy."

Marie Limpert is a professional organizer, event planner and co-owner of Organize Me! of NY, LLC. She is also a Third-Degree Black Belt in Elite Goju Karate. She teaches martial arts and self defense to both adults and children. Prior to becoming a professional organizer, Marie had a successful career in sales management in both the corporate and non-profit sectors. She lives on Long Island with her husband and two children.

After navigating the stressful transition from career women to stay-at-home moms, Annmarie and Marie started Organize Me! of NY, LLC to help other parents in similar transitions. In the past 13 years, their work has expanded to include any person or family looking to improve their situation through better organization. Combining personalized organizing strategies with the science of positive psychology, they help clients reach their goals and create a home and life they love.

Please visit their website at www.organizemeNY.com. Follow them on Instagram and Facebook @organizemeNY.

Endnotes

1   Barbara Frederickson, *Positivity: Top-Notch Research Reveals the Upward Spiral That Will Change Your Life* (New York: Three Rivers Press, 2009), 55–57.

2   Carol S. Dweck, *Mindset: The New Psychology of Success* (New York: Random House, 2006), 70.

3   D. Saddawi-Konefka, D. Schumacher, K. Baker, J. Charnin, and P. Gollwitzer, P., "Changing Physician Behavior With Implementation Intentions: Closing The Gap Between Intentions and Actions," *Academic Medicine* 91, no. 9 (2016): 1211–1216.

4   D. O. Hebb, *The Organization of Behavior: A Psychological Study* (New York: Wiley, 1949).

5   Carol S. Dweck, *Mindset: The New Psychology of Success* (New York: Random House, 2006).

6   Norman Doidge, *The Brain That Changes Itself: Stories of Personal Triumph from the Frontiers of Brain Science* (New York: Penguin Books, 2007).

7   Roy F. Baumeister, Ellen Bratslavsky, Catrin Finkenauer and Kathleen D. Vohs, "Bad Is Stronger Than Good," *Review of General Psychology* 5, no. 4 (2001): 323–370.

8   Carol S. Dweck, *Mindset: The New Psychology of Success* (New York: Random House, 2006), 32–34.

9   Sherrie Bourg Carter, "Why Mess Causes Stress: 8 Reasons, 8 Remedies," *Psychology Today*, March 14, 2012, https://www.psychologytoday.com/us/blog/high-octane-women/201203/why-mess-causes-stress-8-reasons-8-remedies.

10 Andrew Mellen, "Discover the Incredible Power of Decluttering: Get More Out of Your Life By Getting and Staying Organised," *Complete Wellbeing*, December 2013, 24.

11 R. H. Thaler, "Mental Accounting Matters," *Journal of Behavioral Decision Making* 12, no. 3 (1999): 191.

12 C. R. Snyder, "Conceptualising, Measuring and Nurturing Hope," *Journal of Counseling and Development* 73, no. 3 (1995): 355–360.

13 E. Deci, E. and R. Ryan, "Intrinsic Motivation and Self-Determination in Human Behavior," *Perspectives in Social Psychology* (New York: Plenum Press, 1985).

14 G. T. Doran, "There's a S.M.A.R.T. Way to Write Management Goals and Objectives," *Management Review* 70, no. 11 (1981), 35–36.

15 Gail Matthews, Dominican University (2015), https://www.dominican.edu/dominicannews/study-highlights-strategies-for-achieving-goals.

16 Emmie Martin, "23-time gold medalist Michael Phelps uses a simple trick to stay focused on his goals," *CNBC Make It*, January 1, 2019, https://www.cnbc.com/2018/12/20/michael-phelps-strategy-for-reaching-his-goals.html.

17 D. Saddawi-Konefka, D. Schumacher, K. Baker, J. Charnin, and P. Gollwitzer, P., "Changing Physician Behavior With Implementation Intentions: Closing The Gap Between Intentions and Actions," *Academic Medicine* 91, no. 9 (2016): 1211–1216.

18 C. Adams Miller and M. Frisch, *Creating Your Best Life: The Ultimate Life List Guide* (New York: Sterling, 2009), 131–135.

19 For a video on how to create a College Prep Binder, please visit www.organizemeNY.com/videos.

20 Kasser, T., *The High Price of Materialism* (Massachusetts, The MIT Press, 2002).

21 "What Psychology Says About Materialism and the Holidays, Six Questions for materialism expert Tim Kasser, Ph.D," *American Psychological Association*, 2014.

22 Barbara Frederickson, *Positivity: Top-Notch Research Reveals the Upward Spiral That Will Change Your Life* (New York: Random House, 2009), 55–57.

23 Tony Schwartz and Catherine McCarthy, "Manage Your Energy, Not Your Time," *Harvard Business Review*, October 2007, 63–73.

24 Claus Ebster and Marion Garaus, *Store Design and Visual Merchandising: Creating Store Space That Encourages Buying* (New York: Business Expert Press, 2015), 25–26.

25 Ibid, 25–28.

26 Zeigarnik, B. (1927). Das Behalten erledigter und unerledigter Handlungen. *Psychologische Forschung*, 9, 1-85.

27 Ann Landers, "Rules to Live By Are Good as Gold," *Chicago Tribune*, August 1999, 31.

28 Tony Schwartz and Catherine McCarthy, "Manage Your Energy, Not Your Time," *Harvard Business Review*, October 2007, 63–73.

22. Rosabeth Moss Kanter, "Celebrity, IT and Research Foundation Fund: The upward spiral that will enable firm ... big data" (New York Times, Feb. 2009), S.6-7.

23. Eric Schwartz and Catherine McCarthy, "Monkey New Frenzy," Hot ... Ring Financial Bulletin, Score ... October 2007: 85-92.

24. Glenn Llabert and ..., Chains, Client Design and ... Widget mediation, "New Evidence of Team Sensitivity Rating" (New York ... Business Review, 2015): 25-36.

25. Solomon, R. (1991), "Ethics, human emotions and corporate ..." ... Princeton: Ridgeport, Page 4, p.155.

26. ... Ambassador, Angel of Love by ... Corporate Gold, Chicago Tribune, ... August 19, 2012.

27. Tony Schwartz and Catherine McCarthy, "New ... Working ... ..." HBR, May Insight in New ... November September 2007: 57.

Index

Notes

WRITE YOUR GOALS, THOUGHTS, OR REVELATIONS HERE!

Case Studies

We've come to learn that folks just *love* before and after photos. There's something about seeing an amazing transformation that is very inspiring and motivating. In organizing, however, they often don't begin to capture the enormous amount of work and decision-making that is sandwiched in between the before and after.

A picture is worth a thousand words, except when it isn't.

Following are two case studies (a basement storage area and an attic) that we feel encompass the principles we offer in this book. Note that these photos aren't Pinterest worthy. There are no fancy labels or matching decorative bins. They are real pictures taken on our smartphones, and represent the *process* that was used to go from disorganization to organization. The difference between the before and after photos is that our clients have full knowledge of what they have and where to find it when they need it. Their spaces are now maximized and used efficiently, making access to their things effortless and stress-free.

It is our hope that through these photos and descriptions, you will get a really good sense of how these transformations unfolded. All pictures and project details are shared with our clients' permission.

To see all of our case studies and before/after albums in their full color glory (as glorious as smartphone photos can be!), feel free to visit our website at www.organizemeNY.com.

Basement Storage Area

Check out this fabulous basement storage space. Open and spacious, it just needed some focus and planning to maximize its great potential. Our client, who has *no attic, garage, or shed*, depends on this room in a *big* way. She was hard-working and open to seeing the possibilities through our eyes.

Goals: To help our client go through her family's belongings to determine what is still being used. To redesign the room to maximize its storage capacity, as well as to group categories and create associations so our client can easily find what she is looking for at any given moment.

Overall Strategy: We took everything out and sorted it by grouping "like with like." We then helped our client pare down each group as necessary. We set aside things for an upcoming garage sale, packed up donations, threw out anything that was broken or missing pieces, and relocated anything that belonged in other areas of the home. We then took what was left and re-organized the space to create clear zones for the different categories of items. We based these decisions on convenience, frequency of use, client preference, and size/weight.

The End Result: An efficient and aesthetically pleasing storage area with clear zones and easy accessibility to the things our client needs.

BEFORE: Even before entering the room, you can tell from the doorway that this is a great space. What it lacked was different zones. It also had started to become a bit of a dumping ground, which happens when things do not have a designated home.

AFTER: Now *this* makes us want to enter the room. Things are off the floor, and our client knows exactly which part of the room to go to depending on what she is looking for. For example, need a piece of luggage? No searching required. It's all in one place straight ahead.

BEFORE: Turn the corner to the left and surprise—so much room! But it was filled with things on the floor that made it hard to get around. And notice all that unused wall space! We saw the potential immediately.

AFTER: Look at the difference! By repositioning some of the storage racks, we maximized the useable wall space and designated a "home" for all the categories in the room: gardening, housewares, outdoor/bbq, overflow items, holiday decorations, utility, gift wrap. Now when you turn the corner, there's a clear path and easy access to whatever our client needs.

BEFORE: This rack was filled to capacity, and yet wasn't serving our client well at all. There wasn't a clear purpose for the piece, and it wasn't easy to access anything without the risk of things falling. It was very easy to lose sight (literally and figuratively) of what was in the back.

AFTER: For aesthetics, we swapped out the chrome rack with a white one our client had. This unit is right near the room's entrance, so we placed often-accessed categories here: water bottles, pet food, and gift wrapping. No need to even go far into the room to get what they look for most often!

BEFORE: Our client had the right idea here, allocating this space for outdoor and gardening. It is very challenging when you don't have a garage, attic, or shed! But look at all that unused wall space on the side. And there were miscellaneous items mixed in there, too.

AFTER: We just built on her foundation, regrouping the winter and gardening tools so that even the hanging items have a system. We also added the other chrome rack to maximize the unused wall space and relocated the miscellaneous items to their appropriate homes based on category. If the category didn't yet exist elsewhere in the space, we created one and established a home for it.

Walk-Up Attic

Here are some before and after photos of a walk-up attic. Our client is a successful and extremely busy attorney, as well as a hands-on mom and president of a very active non-profit organization.

Goal: Our client's vision was to use her attic to store specific categories of her belongings: keepsake items, furniture, and decorating items for future use, seasonal clothing, luggage, and the extensive amount of supplies needed to run her foundation and its many events. The Foundation was established in memory of her late husband, an FDNY and local firefighter and 9/11 first responder who passed away in 2009 from 9/11-related cancer. In organizing this space, we knew we would come across very sentimental and emotional belongings. Our goal was to make this project as least overwhelming as possible, and to help our client feel safe and supported with compassion and respect.

Overall Strategy: Since our client already had very clear preferences and a strong vision for the space, we put our energy into making the process itself as efficient and stress-free as possible. There were a significant amount of bins and boxes that needed to be opened and sorted through. We grouped "like with like" and helped our client pare down the different categories. She was great about making decisions and balancing her sentimentality with her vision and goals for the space. She donated a good amount and only kept things she really loves or is still using. This gave us more room to use for organizing the space. As you will read below, the area was zoned very specifically based on our client's preferences and needs.

The End Result: A functional and uncluttered space that effectively stores both personal belongings and professional materials in a way that's convenient and easily accessible.

STAIRWAY/ENTRY–BEFORE. Our client (who is very organized, by the way), was very specific about what she wanted the space to be. The unsightly clutter in this photo was causing stress, and it was important to clear the area at the top of the stairs so that it was more visually appealing. She also knew that she wanted certain foundation materials to be immediately accessible, while others could be housed farther back in the room.

STAIRWAY/ENTRY–AFTER. Right off the bat, you can see that the clutter has been cleared and things are in order. Straight ahead are foundation event supplies that don't need to be accessed on a regular basis. However, to the left are things that are accessed regularly, allowing our client to get to them without really even entering the space. Also, we cleared the stairs for safe travel up and down, and found homes for some "For Now" clutter that had been just "hanging out" there.

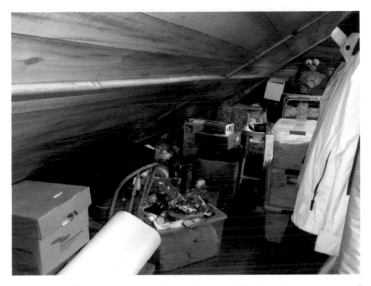

LEFT SIDE–BEFORE. This side was filled with a mixture of keepsakes, foundation stuff, furniture, old toys, etc. We did what we always do–we went through everything. We threw out anything that was broken or missing pieces. Our client was great at making decisions about what could be donated and what needed to stay. Everything that remained was sorted and packed up in clearly labeled bins.

LEFT SIDE–AFTER. The slanted roof of many attics makes storage difficult, because you can only stack so many bins on top of each other. We used this space for foundation materials that are only accessed when a particular event is happening (vs. materials that are used regularly throughout the year). For this reason, we allowed certain bins to be placed in front of others.

RIGHT SIDE–BEFORE. This side contained luggage, old paperwork, change-of-season clothing, and miscellaneous "stuff." But there were also very personal keepsake items which were *not* easy to go through, including things from 9/11. This required extreme care and compassion. We remain humbled and honored at the trust our client placed in us with regard to this task.

RIGHT SIDE–AFTER. We grouped "like with like," and then went through each category, breaking down this big project into smaller, more manageable tasks for our client to handle. We then placed keepsake items towards the back. Although you can't see it in this picture, change of season clothing, luggage, and travel items were placed right near the entry and clearly labeled so they can be accessed quickly and easily without having to go too far into the room.